Speaker's Complete Library of Wit and Humor

BILL ADLER

Speaker's Complete Library of Wit and Humor

BILL ADLER

Parker Publishing Company, Inc.
West Nyack, New York

© 1970, BY

PARKER PUBLISHING COMPANY, INC.
WEST NYACK, NEW YORK

LIBRARY OF CONGRESS
CATALOG CARD NUMBER: 79-119851

AUG 12 '71

PRINTED IN THE UNITED STATES OF AMERICA

ISBN-0-13-824078-7
ENCYCLOPEDIA

How to Get the Most Out of Bill Adler's

SPEAKER'S COMPLETE LIBRARY OF WIT AND HUMOR

Using the "Master Index" and the "Speaker's Log"

You already know that one guaranteed way to hit it off with an audience is to leaven your remarks with *humor*—humor that's right for the occasion, the audience, and for the point you're making.

You know this—or why else would you have sought out this SPEAKER'S COMPLETE LIBRARY OF WIT AND HUMOR?

So, let's take a few moments to see how quickly, how easily, how directly you can come up with the *right* rib-tickling, point-driving quotation—starting with the

MASTER INDEX

In sports, you can tell the players by the numbers. In speakers' quote books, though there are usually plenty of numbers, but you still can't tell the *jokes*. In most of them, you look up the topic, and get a wide assortment of "entry numbers" sending you all over the book. Each quote to which you are referred has to be read through; how else would you decide which "entry" to use in your talk? In *this* book, not so—you get the gist of the gag right in the MASTER INDEX (placed first because it's the natural starting point in using the "Library").

Because every entry—every anecdote, bon mot, conundrum, drollery, right on to "zinger"—has its own individual *caption* to tell you in an instant what the entry is about. And you get the *caption* in the MASTER INDEX.

That's one way the SPEAKER'S COMPLETE LIBRARY OF WIT AND HUMOR stands up and delivers faster and better than other sourcebooks of humor. Another way it helps you to more effective public speaking is in its

SPEAKER'S LOG

If you speak even only occasionally, you must have had this nightmare: you're telling a story to an audience, you know it's a real crowd-pleaser because you've broken up audiences with it before, and yet as you go on you can see your listeners' eyes grow glassy, their attention drifting away. And then you realize—in your nightmare—*you've told the same story before, to the same audience.*

THE SPEAKER'S LOG—appearing on the tabbed opening pages for each of the "Library" sections—makes it absolutely impossible for the nightmare to come true. You can't tell the same audience the same joke because you have entered into the log the entry number, the date, and the audience for every anecdote, bon mot, etc. you use.

Then again, you might have experienced that sinking feeling of just never getting it off the ground. Here, the LIBRARY again comes to your rescue with a complete section devoted exclusively to openers—and on just about any subject you can name from Baldness to Fund Raising.

51243

Put the LIBRARY to work the next time you are asked to deliver a few well chosen remarks. In seconds you will be convinced that this is a SPEAKER'S LIBRARY that has been designed *to be used* and stands *ready to deliver* on virtually any subject you can name.

Bill Adler now presents the collection of his career—ready for you to put to work and avoid many of the pitfalls summed up by George Bernard Shaw when asked how he had developed his gift for oratory, "I learned to speak as men learn to skate or cycle, by doggedly making a fool of myself until I got used to it." With SPEAKER'S LIBRARY you need not have this experience.

MASTER INDEX

F

H

Q

R

T

FAST STARTS

1001 A WIT

"I might as well state before I begin that I am not going to try and be too funny tonight. I believe that a man who thinks himself a wit is usually half right."

1002 SHARP TONGUE AND DULL MIND

"I have been looking forward to speaking to you tonight and I sincerely hope when I am finished that you won't say that a sharp tongue and a dull mind are usually found in the same head!"

1003 FIRST DATE

"As I begin tonight, I sort of feel like the young boy who went out on his first date with a girl. It wasn't that he didn't know what to do, but that he didn't know where to begin."

1004 BIKINI—TOP OF

"My speech tonight will be like the top of a bikini. It will cover only the high spots."

1005 BALDNESS

"My speech tonight will be like baldness—not much there—but neat."

1006 LOVE LETTER

"I have always believed that an after-dinner speech is like a love letter. Ideally,

1

you should begin by not knowing what you are going to say and end by not knowing what you've said."

1007   PROFOUND SPEECH

"I would like to open by saying that I hope you find my speech profound. When both the speaker and the audience are confused, a speech is profound."

1008   HOW TO STAY AWAKE

"The easiest way to stay awake during an after-dinner speech is to deliver it."

1009   PUBLIC SPEAKING—FUTILITY OF

"Accustomed as I am to public speaking, I know the futility of it."

1010   GRACEFUL SPEAKER—DEFINITION OF

"I hope that I don't fall into the definition of a 'graceful speaker'—that being one who can say nothing in the most words."

1011   AFTER-DINNER SPEECH—CALLED ON TO MAKE

"There is but one pleasure in life equal to that of being called on to make an after-dinner speech, and that is not being called on to make one."

1012   CLOSING REMARKS—BEGINNING OF SPEECH

"Ladies and gentlemen, I would like to begin my speech with my closing remarks for those of you who have to leave early."

1013   CONGRATULATIONS

"First, I want to publicly congratulate those who had the good sense to stay home tonight."

1014   AD-LIB SPEECH—REPEATED

"I hope that you enjoy my ad-lib speech tonight. This is the third time I have given it."

1015 FLATTERING INTRODUCTIONS—EFFECT OF

"I love flattering introductions. Flattering introductions are like smoking. They don't hurt you if you don't inhale."

1016 CHRISTMAS PAGEANT—FATHER'S PART IN

"As I stand here before this crowd, knowing what an intelligent group you are, I feel somewhat like a phony. I'm reminded of the little boy whose father was in the Christmas pageant. 'What part does your father have?' somebody asked him. He answered proudly, 'He's one of the Wise Guys from the East.' "

1017 FLATTERY—SNIFFED NOT SWALLOWED

"Hearing this marvelous and gracious introduction tonight I am reminded that flattery is like perfume—it is to be sniffed and not swallowed."

1018 AMERICAN PUBLIC DINNER—DESCRIPTION OF

"The American public dinner has been described by a popular after-dinner speaker as 'an affair where a speaker first eats a lot of food he doesn't want then proceeds to talk about something he doesn't understand to a lot of people who don't want to hear him.' "

1019 INSTRUMENTS FOR THROWING SPEAKERS VOICE—FOR THROWING SPEAKER

"I understand that instruments have been invented that will throw a speaker's voice more than a mile. Now what we need is an instrument that will throw the speaker an equal distance."

1020 HAPPY ENDING

"Almost every after-dinner speech has a happy ending—everybody is glad when it's over."

1021 IMPROVING AFTER-DINNER SPEECH

"The best way to improve an after-dinner speech is to...shorten it!"

1022 COOPERATION AND KINDNESS

"Today I ask you for kindness and cooperation as we approach this difficult subject—like the Wisconsin housewife who cured her husband's snoring. She said that she had used cooperation and kindness—and then stuffed an old sock in his mouth!"

1023 SPEAKING FREE OF CHARGE

"As I think of the speech I am about to give tonight, I also think of the toast-master who prepared the audience for the speaker by remarking, 'And remember —he's speaking free of charge.' "

1024 LETTER OF INVITATION—OPENED BY MISTAKE

"When your letter of invitation arrived, it had a note on the envelope which said, 'opened by mistake.' After you've heard me, you may wish that the original opener had just throw it away!"

1025 CHURCH JANITOR—I STILL BELIEVE IN GOD

"You know, I do expect you to take my speech in stride. You are the kind of folks who have a good idea of where you stand. I'm thinking of the church janitor who said, 'I've seen twelve preachers come and go, and I still believe in God.' "

1026 ESSENTIAL FACTS

"My speech tonight will stick to the essential facts. Not at all like the two fellows who were standing on the street corner talking to each other. One fellow turned to the other and said, 'I won't bore you with any more details. In fact, I've already told you more than I heard myself.' "

1027 MODEST SPEAKER

"You are fortunate in having such a modest speaker today. I may have my faults—but being wrong is not one of them."

1028 GOAL—THINK

"My goal tonight is to make you think. You've all heard of the fellow who came home from the office looking tired and haggard and his wife said to him, 'How was it at the office, dear?' He replied, 'Terrible. The computer stopped and we all had to think.' "

1029   MEANINGFUL SPEECH—HOLLOW

"I trust that you will find my speech meaningful tonight. Not like the two boys who were watching a fat woman mount a scale, which was actually out of order, and when the needle stopped at sixty-four pounds one of the boys exclaimed, 'Look at that. She's hollow!' "

1030   FRIENDS

"It is my desire that we remain friends during my speech, in the manner of the child who was playing with a worm in the back yard and cut the worm in two. As each end wriggled vigorously the child remarked, 'There. Now you have a friend!' "

1031   PERFECT—ONE MORE TIME, BETTER

"Let's hope you don't make the same comment at the close of my speech that the Hollywood director made after a scene had just been shot, 'Perfect. Perfect. Now let's do it over one more time—better.' "

1032   WANTED

"When I was asked by your chairman to speak here today I asked him if he was sure that he really wanted me. I reminded him of the sign put over the door of the Kansas City Marriage License Bureau, 'Out to lunch. Think it over.' "

1033   EARLY TO BED AND EARLY TO RISE

"May I first offer you some words of advice: 'Early to bed and early to rise and you'll meet very few prominent people.' "

1034   AGNOSTICS—HEARING OF

"I hope you will all be able to hear me. There was once a visiting clergyman in an English church who asked advice of the custodian. 'Speak loudly,' he advised, 'the agnostics hear poorly.' "

1035   AN AUTHOR AND A SPEAKER—DIFFERENCE BETWEEN

"Of course, you all know the difference between an author and a speaker. An author is a man you can shut up by closing a book."

1036   **SUITABLE SPEECH—SIMPLE**

"Before I came here tonight I asked my wife what sort of speech she thought would best suit my personality and she replied, 'Simple.' "

1037   **PEOPLE SITTING THROUGH AFTER-DINNER SPEECHES**

"If all the people who sit through after-dinner speeches were lined up three feet apart—they would stretch."

1038   **LATE—EXCUSE FOR BEING**

When you are late, try this opener:
"A teacher asked a little girl why she was five minutes late for school. 'I must have overwashed,' she replied."

1039   **ORIGINAL SCHEDULED SPEECH—DELIVERY OF**

"I have bad news for you tonight, friends. The speech that I was originally scheduled to deliver—I am going to go ahead and give anyway."

1040   **INTRODUCTION—BELIEVING WORDS**

"Thank you for those very kind and flattering words of introduction. I believe every word."

1041   **ARRIVING LATE FOR SPEECH**

If you are late in arriving to make your speech, you can start off with, "I'm sorry I am late. I am reminded that when Eve saw Adam for the first time in the Garden of Eden she probably asked him if he had been waiting long."

1042   **LOUDSPEAKER—DONATION OF**

"I want to congratulate you on your excellent public speaking equipment. There was once a pastor in Texas who announced to the congregation that the church had acquired a new public address system. 'The microphone and the wiring were paid out of church funds,' the pastor explained, 'but the loud-speaker was donated by one of our members in memory of his late wife.' "

1043   **FRATERNAL ORGANIZATION—SPEAKING BEFORE**

If you are speaking before a fraternal organization, "Did you hear about the little boy who boasted to a classmate, 'My father is an Elk, a Lion and a Moose.' 'Gee,' replied the other kid, 'How much does it cost to get a look at him?' "

1044 INTRODUCTION—LONG

Following a long introduction, "Good evening, ladies and gentlemen. Do I have time to say anything more?"

1045 SALESMEN—GIVING SPEECH TO

When giving a speech to salesmen, "The best sales talk I ever heard belongs to the door-to-door salesman who opens every pitch with, 'I've got an item here that your next door neighbor tells me you can't afford.' "

1046 RIPPING UP YOUR SPEECH—PRETENDING

Rip some papers up—as though you were ripping up your speech—and then say, "Believe me friends, you wouldn't have liked that speech anyway."

1047 LATENESS—SLOW DOG

If you are late, "I guess I could use the excuse of the little boy who was asked by the teacher why he was late for school one day. 'Well,' he replied, 'I was walking behind a very slow dog.' "

1048 THE WINNER

Hold up a $10.00 bill (or a $5.00 bill) and announce, "This goes to the last man to fall asleep."

1049 PRAYING

Fold your hands in front of you as if in prayer and say, "I'm with you, folks. I'm praying it's a good speech, too."

1050 BRIGHT AND ALERT AUDIENCE—SPEAKING TO

"Ladies and gentlemen, It's a real pleasure to be here. The last time I spoke to such a bright and alert audience was when, standing in front of a mirror, I spoke to myself."

1051   TOGETHERNESS

Start your speech on one foot and then remark, "I guess if *you're* going to suffer, we ought to suffer together."

1052   PUTTING THE AUDIENCE TO SLEEP

"Good evening, folks. I promise not to keep you awake too long."

1053   AUDIENCES—ALLEGIC TO

Blow your nose forcefully a few times and quip, "You'll have to excuse me, friends, but I'm allergic to audiences."

1054   DEAFENING APPLAUSE

Hold your hands over your ears and then remark, "I hope you don't mind but I find all this applause deafening."

1055   WIFE'S TWO WORDS OF ADVICE

"Before I left home tonight, my wife gave me two words of advice—'DON'T GO!' "

1056   COMMENTS IN AUDIENCE BEFORE SPEECH

"I certainly appreciate some of the comments I heard in the audience before I came up here to speak—but I've decided to go ahead, anyway."

1057   ONLY OPPORTUNITY TO SMILE

Smile broadly and then quip to your audience. "I always like to *start* my speeches with a smile—it may be my only opportunity."

1058   MAN'S BAD LUCK—STREAK OF

"There's one man in our audience who remarked that he had never missed any of my speeches. But when he was asked why this was so, he answered, 'Just a streak of bad luck, I guess!' "

1059   WRONG NIGHT—SPEAKING ON

"I love to speak before bright, intelligent, alert and attractive audiences but I guess this just isn't the night."

1060   AUDIENCE WILL BELIEVE ANYTHING

"Ladies and gentlemen: Let me begin by saying that it is a real pleasure to be here. Now...if you believe that, you'll believe anything I'm going to say tonight."

1061   AUDIENCE—TEST OF

Close your eyes as you are about to speak and say, "Now, friends, the real test of a good audience is...will you still be there when I open my eyes at the conclusion of my speech."

1062   WEARING APPAREL

"I was going to wear my good suit tonight but I didn't want you folks to feel out of place."

1063   REQUEST DURING SPEECH—QUIET PLEASE

"I have only one request during my speech, ladies and gentlemen. I must have absolute quiet. So please, no unnecessary breathing."

1064   COUGH SESSION BEFORE SPEECH

Cough a few times and then say to your audience, "Won't you all please join me in a good cough now—*before* I begin."

1065   ATTENTIVE AUDIENCE

"It's a great thrill to speak before such an attentive audience. Last time I spoke to such an attentive audience was at Forest Law Cemetary."

1066   RELAYING SPEECH

"Good evening, friends. If at any time during my speech tonight you understand what I am talking about, please be a sport and inform the person sitting next to you. They'll appreciate it!"

1067 ATTENTIVE AUDIENCES

"The last time I addressed such an attentive audience was when I spoke at Sing Sing."

1068 TRADING AUDIENCES

"You're a wonderful audience and I wouldn't trade you for any other audience in the world—but I sure wish I had the chance."

1069 PROFILE—CHOICE OF

Stand with your left profile toward the audience then turn so that your right profile faces the audience and then remark, "You have your choice, folks. Do you like my left or right profile best—I can speak either way."

1070 BRIEF REMARKS—REASON FOR

"My remarks are going to be very brief. I have given up long speeches on account of my throat. I don't want anybody to cut it."

1071 GREETING MIXED AUDIENCE

"Good evening, ladies and gentlemen. And those of you who are neither."

OPENING SHOCKERS

1072 PRICELESS SPEECH

"Usually I am a very modest person, but today I am going to begin my speech by letting you in on a little secret. The speech I am about to give is really priceless. And when I say my speech is priceless I mean that it costs you nothing and is worth every penny of it."

1073 A PLEDGE TO LISTEN

Raise your right hand and say to your audience, "Now repeat after me. I promise to faithfully listen...."

1074 SAD LOOKING

Look very sad and remark, "I know how sad I look but it's not for me that I am sad—I was just thinking of you."

1075 LOVING ME

Throw a big 'Dinah Shore' kiss to your audience and quip, "Will you love me at the finish like you do when I begin?"

1076 DRINKING WATER

Take a drink of water and quip, "If you think this is water you're more drunk *now* than I'll be when I *finish*."

1077 WEARING SAME TIE

"Will the gentleman in the audience who is wearing the same tie that I am please remove his immediately."

1078   BLINKING—REASON FOR

Blink your eyes noticeably a few times and quip. "I want to apologize for blinking like this but I am blinded by all this beauty."

1079   MIXED EMOTIONS

Smile, then look sad, and then smile again and say, "I can't decide whether to be happy or sad about being here."

1080   SPEAKER'S ANNOUNCEMENT

Cover your eyes with your hands and announce, "Now when I count to three, everybody throw a $10.00 bill to the speaker."

1081   BEFORE SPEECH—GETTING NAMES OF PEOPLE IN AUDIENCE

Take out a pen from your pocket and begin to write on a piece of paper and then remark, "I start my speech in a few seconds, gentlemen, but first the Internal Revenue Service wanted me to send them the names of each of you in the audience here tonight."

1082   BASEBALL GAME—PRIZE FOR BREVITY

"The prize for brevity should go to the grade school pupil who gave a speech about a baseball game. He arose and said, 'Rain. No game.' "

1083   STRIKING OIL—TIME FOR

"A speaker who does not strike oil in twenty minutes should stop boring."

1084   GOOD SPEECH—CLOSENESS OF

"A good speech has a good beginning and a good ending, and both should be kept very close together."

1085   CHAIRMAN—EXIT OF

"I want to thank your chairman for the confidence he has placed in me tonight. I would also like to announce that he has just left quickly through the nearest exit."

1086   EMPTY HANDED AND MATCHING HEAD

"I came here tonight empty handed and with a head to match!"

1087   PUBLIC SPEAKER'S WEEK—DECLARATION OF

"Before I begin my speech, I would just like to say that this has been declared National Be Kind to Public Speakers Week."

1088   CHAIRMAN'S REMARKS—LISTENER'S OBITUARY

"Thank you, Mr. Chairman. I didn't realize—until I just listened to your remarks—that my obituary had already been written."

1089   WORLD'S BEST AFTER-DINNER SPEECH

"No matter how good my speech is, it won't be the world's best after dinner speech, which always is: 'Waiter, I'll take the check!' "

1090   SPEECH—SIZE OF

"My speech tonight will be like a mini-skirt. Long enough to cover most of the subject but short enough to be interesting."

1091   FEW APPROPRIATED WORDS

"What I have to say, I will say in a few appropriated words."

1092   CHAIRMAN'S BUILD-UP—TALK AFTER

"After such a terrific build-up by the chairman, I can hardly wait to hear what I have to say."

1093   SPEAKER LIKE TEXAN

"As I speak to you tonight, please don't be too hard on me. I am like the Texan who said, "I really don't lie—I just remember big."

1094   SALESMEN—SPEAKING BEFORE

When speaking before salesmen, "May I first offer you this definition of a salesman. A fellow with a smile on his face, a shine on his shoes, and 'a lousy territory.' "

1095   PAYING LITTLE ATTENTION

"I hope you'll pay attention to my speech tonight—not however, like the little boy in school who was told by the teacher to pay a little attention. 'I'm paying as little attention as I can,' he said."

1096   UNSUCCESSFUL SPEECH—REASON FOR

"One speaker said that he gave a completely successful speech to an audience. It was soothing (the people slept) and moving (half of them got up and left) and satisfying (they didn't come back). By that definition I shall try and be a failure by keeping you awake, and keeping you here."

1097   HONESTY—STORY ABOUT

"I am going to try and keep my speech honest tonight. My favorite story about honesty concerns the magician who called a small boy up on the stage to assist in his act, saying, 'Now my boy—you've never seen me before?' 'No, Daddy.' "

1098   EVENING'S FORMAL DINNER—INSTRUCTIONS TO MAID

"I thought this story might set the tone for my speech tonight. The lady of the house was instructing the maid for the evening's formal dinner. 'Now, Mary, when you are serving tonight be careful and don't spill anything.' To which the maid answered, 'Don't worry, ma'am. I never talk too much.' "

1099   ADVICE FROM SON

Raise your hands as if in prayer and quip, "Right before I came here today I asked my son what was the first thing I should do before I start to speak, and he replied, 'Pray, Dad, pray!' "

1100   AN ANSWER TO YOUR PRAYERS

"I hope my speech tonight is the answer to your prayers. There was once a young preacher, unmarried, who was doing a great job rounding up members. He was pleased to see a young widow among the worshippers one morning. 'I want to welcome you,' the minister said, 'I prayed for you the other night for a whole hour.' 'Why didn't you give me a buzz?' she replied, 'I could have been over in ten minutes.' "

1101   INTERESTING PROPOSITION

"My only desire tonight is that you will find my speech interesting—like the man who received a note which read, '$1000 or we kidnap your wife.' 'I don't have the money,' he replied, 'but your proposition interests me.' "

1102   WHAT IS A BANQUET?

"It is a pleasure to be here at this banquet. I am sure you all know what a banquet is. It's a $2.00 dinner served in sufficient numbers to enable the caterer to charge $10 for it."

1103   FUND RAISING DINNER

Opener for a fund raising dinner, "Thank you, ladies and gentlemen. I was very touched by your warm introduction but not as touched as you will be when the speeches are over."

1104   REHEARSED SPEECH

"I want to tell you honestly that I rehearsed my speech a few times before I came here. I felt like the out-of-towner who asked the New Yorker, "How can I get to Carnegie Hall?' The New Yorker replied, 'Practice.' "

1105   AUDITIONING AUDIENCES

"As you know, I do quite a lot of public speaking and tonight I'm auditioning audiences to take with me to Paris, London and Hawaii."

1106   A STRANGE BEGINNING

Begin with, "Good evening, Ladies and Gentlemen—you are all under arrest."

1107   GRANDFATHER'S ADVICE ON PUBLIC SPEAKING

"The best advice I have ever heard concerning public speaking came from my grandfather who once told me, 'Only speak as long as you are making sense and talking facts,' so in following my grandfather's advice I say to you, Good Night, Folks." (Move as though you were going to sit down.)

1108   WOMEN—WHEN SPEAKING TO

When you are addressing a group of women only, "What a pleasure it is for me to speak to the finalists of the Miss America pageant."

1109   PREPARED SPEECH

"The average 'prepared speech' at a banquet is like the fellow who worked for six months forging a check only to have it come back marked 'Insufficient Funds.' "

1110   UNIONS—LABOR

When speaking before a labor (or business) organization, "I guess you all know how a union man starts a bedtime story to his child, 'Once upon a time and a half...' "

1111   THE FIGHTING SPEAKER

Take off your jacket and turn to your audience and say, "Anyone who walks out on my speech will have to deal with me personally."

1112   JOKES—LAUGHING AT

"I want you to know that you are under no obligation to laugh during my speech. Not at all like the boss who returned to the office after a two martini lunch and got all the secretaries together to tell them a couple of jokes. All the secretaries laughed except one. 'What's the matter,' the boss said to her, 'don't you have a sense or humor?' She replied, 'I don't have to laugh. I'm leaving Friday.' "

1113   NO WATCH—SIX HOURS TO GO

Look at your watch and then say to your audience, "My watch stopped. Will somebody please tell me when my six hours are up."

1114   INTRODUCTIONS—THANK YOU FOR

"Thank you for that fine introduction. That was the second best introduction I've ever had. The best was once when the dinner chairman was missing and I had to introduce myself."

1115   SPEAKER—FIRST ONE TO RUN

Run in place in front of your audience and say, "I thought I would get a head start in case you don't like my speech."

1116   SPEAKER'S WIFE—ABSENCE OF

"My wife wanted to be here tonight but when she found out who the speaker was going to be, she discovered she was busy this evening."

1117   CHANCE TO TALK

"I certainly appreciate the opportunity to come here and speak to you tonight. You see, I don't get a chance to talk too often—I've been married for 25 years."

1118   MASS RALLY OUTSIDE AFTER SPEECH—REASON FOR

"Ladies and gentlemen, immediately after my speech there will be a mass rally outside—to call for the arrest of the program chairman."

1119   ACTING—SPEAKER, AUDIENCE, AND HOLD-UP MEN

Begin by whistling and acting as if you were trying to be very casual, "Act like nothing is happening, folks, and maybe the holdup men in the rear will go away quietly."

1120   GOOD NIGHT—AS OPENER

"Ladies and gentlemen, I would like to open with just two words—GOOD NIGHT!" And then move as if you were leaving the platform or going to sit down.

1121   WARNING BY SPEAKER TO AUDIENCE

"I would like to mention first of all that immediately after this speech—I am going to have a nervous collapse."

1122   STRETCHING TIME OF SPEECH

Start your speech by talking very slowly and then remark, "I hope you don't mind, folks, but I'm trying to make a two minute speech last for an hour."

1123   BUSINESS GROUP—SPEAKING BEFORE

"On my way over here tonight I saw an interesting sign in a store window. It read 'You can fool some of the people some of the time, and generally speaking, that's enough to allow for a profit.' "

1124   PREPAREDNESS

"Is there a doctor in the house? Nobody feels sick now—but we ought to be prepared."

1125   LEFT SPEECH AT HOME

"Ladies and gentlemen, it is with a great deal of pride and pleasure that I tell you that. . .I left my speech at home."

1126   BLOCKING GETAWAY CAR

"Will the person driving the car with the license plate number 6Z4972 please remove your auto from out front. You're blocking my getaway car."

1127   CONGRATULATIONS IN ORDER

"Good evening, friends. First I would like to congratulate your program chairman on his good taste in the selection of your speaker today."

1128   MY LIFE—HAPPIEST MOMENT OF

"Ladies and gentlemen, being here tonight is the happiest moment of my life. Which just goes to show you what kind of rough times I've had."

1129   FLAT SPEAKER

"I am going to make my remarks **brief and** to the point because I know that a speaker, like ginger ale, goes flat a few **minutes** after being uncorked."

1130   WHAT I THINK AND BELIEVE—NOT WHAT I KNOW

"Ladies and gentlemen, I am going to tell you what I think and believe. If I tell you what I know, I would immediately have to sit right down."

MORE ATTENTION GETTERS

1131   EXPRESSION—ART OF

"Public speaking is the art of expressing a two minute idea with a two hour vocabulary."

1132   THE WHISPERING SPEECH

Begin by speaking very softly and almost in a whisper say to your audience, "Can you hear me all right?"

1133   LIP MOVEMENT—TO QUIET AUDIENCE

Move your lips as though you are speaking—but make no sounds. This is guaranteed to quiet your audience.

1134   THE SINGING SPEAKER

Open your speech by singing a few bars of the *Star Spangled Banner* and then quip, "For my next number I would like to do . . ."

1135   GETTING A HEAD START

Applaud for a few seconds and then quip, "I just thought I'd start the ball rolling."

1136   WAY TO AWAKEN AUDIENCE BEFORE STARTING SPEECH

Raise your right hand and announce, "Will everybody please raise their right hand. Thank you. Now please raise your left hand. Thank you. Now please raise both hands together. Thank you. I just like to make sure my audience is awake *before* I start."

1137   DISTRACTED BY SPEAKER'S BEAUTY

Turn your back to the audience and then remark, "Why should I keep you distracted from my speech by my natural beauty" or "Now you are looking at the best part of me."

1138   ATTENTIVE AUDIENCE

"I know that you'll be an attentive audience. Not like the father who said to his son, "How many times have I told you never to interrupt your mother when she's listening.'"

1139   BAD NEWS—MICROPHONE WORKING

Tap the microphone a few times and quip, "Ladies and gentlemen, I have bad news for you. The microphone *is* working."

1140   FIRST QUESTION

Take out a cigarette, put it in your mouth and say, "First, let me ask this important question—does anybody have a match?"

1141   BULL ROLLING—AN AFTER-DINNER SPEAKER'S

"An after-dinner speaker is the fellow who starts the bull rolling."

1142   ANOTHER SPEAKER

"My friends, take heart:
    It's never so bleak
    That it can't be bleaker—
    There might have been
    Another speaker!"

1143   AFTER-DINNER SPEAKER

"As I stand here before you, I am reminded of the known medical fact that, temporarily the sense of hearing is considerably dulled by eating. It seems that nature is very kind to us and does the best she can to protect us against after-dinner speakers!"

1144   STARTING SPEECH—ANXIETY

"I'm going to start my speech right away. I'm as anxious as you are to hear what I have to say."

1145   STUFFED FISH—ADVICE GIVEN BY

"I may take the advice given by that poor stuffed fish which was mounted on the wall and under it was this sign, 'If I had kept my mouth shut, I wouldn't be here.' "

1146   SILENCE IS GOLDEN

"It is better to remain silent and appear a fool, than to speak and remove all doubt."

1147   AMPLIFIERS—RESULT OF

"The great difficulty in amplifiers is that they amplify the speaker's voice, but not his ideas."

1148   APPLAUSE—FAITH, HOPE AND CHARITY

"There are three applause periods in a speech. The audience's applause at the beginning of the speech expresses faith. Applause in the middle of the speech expresses hope. Applause at the end of the speech expresses charity."

1149   SPOUTING BABY WHALE—DANGER OF

" 'Remember', said the mama whale to her child, 'that when you are spouting, you are in most danger of being harpooned.' "

1150   OFF-THE-CLIFF REMARKS

Look attentively at the cuff of your shirt and quip, "I would like to start off tonight with a few off-the-cuff remarks."

1151   CONDENSED REMARKS

"My remarks today will be like the milk you get in cans—condensed."

1152   STILL SPEAKING

"Unaccustomed as I am to public speaking—I still do it!"

1153   SPEECH—FACULTY OF MAN

"Speech is the faculty given to man to conceal his thoughts."

1154   BRIEF REMARKS—ALLOWANCE OF WORDS

"I'm sorry but my remarks must be especially brief. You see, my wife has me on an allowance of five hundred words a day."

1155   OPEN-MINDED PEOPLE—PREJUDICED MAN

"You people here at —— have a wonderful reputation for being openminded. That's good. I once heard of a man who was so prejudiced that he wouldn't even listen to both sides of a phonograph record."

1156   LAUGHING AT JOKES

"I hope you'll laugh at my jokes as they occur. But please don't laugh before they are finished. An African interpreter got tired of a long funny story being told by a speaker. So he finally said, 'He tells jokes. Laugh.' They all did."

1157   SOUND IDEAS—SPEECH

"I hope that you don't say about my speech tonight, 'His ideas are sound— all sound!' "

1158   BRIEF WORDS—WORLD'S SHORTEST PLAY

"My words will be brief tonight, but not as brief as the world's shortest play: Act I, Lion and Two Hunters. Act II, Lion and One Hunter. Act III, Lion."

1159   QUALIFICATION—CALL FOR HELP

"I certainly pray that you find me qualified to make this speech today. Not at all like the shy young man who finally got up the courage to say to his girl, 'If I tried to kiss you, would you call for help?' She quickly replied, 'Why, do you need help?' "

1160   ALL IS SAID AND DONE

"Someone has said that when all is said and done—there will usually be more said than done."

1161   SERVICE—REACTION OF CONGREGATION

"I would hate to see this story applicable to my speech here tonight. It's about the minister who asked his son, 'Do you think the congregation reacted favorably to my message this morning?' 'I'm sure of it, Dad,' the son replied, 'I saw several of them nodding all through the service.' "

1162   HELIUM, RADIUM, AND TEDIUM—DISCOVERY OF

"It took Sir William Ramsey sixteen years to discover helium; the Curies, thirty years to find radium, but in twenty minutes a poor public speaker can produce tedium."

1163   ACCURACY—MANNER OF

"Tonight I will try and be accurate, but not at all in the manner to the newspaper in Kansas that advertises itself as: 'First with the correction.' "

1164   FINE SPEECH—MISSED OPPORTUNITIES TO SIT DOWN

"After my last speech, I asked my wife who was in the audience, how I had done. She said, 'Fine. Only you missed several opportunities to sit down.' "

1165   PUBLIC SPEAKING MOTTO

"My public speaking motto is:
A speech that's full of sparkling wit,
Will keep its hearers grinning,
Provided that the end of it is close to the beginning."

1166   OPENING PRAYER

"May I open with a prayer:
Lord, fill my mouth with worthwhile stuff,
And nudge me when I've said enough."

1167   THREE SIDES TO EVERY STORY

"Just remember, friends, that there are three sides to every story—his, yours, and the truth."

1168   QUESTIONS AFTER SPEECH

"Good evening, folks. Please pay close attention—I'm going to ask questions later."

1169   CLOSING SPEECH BEFORE AN OPENER

Open your speech saying, "And in conclusion—let me say . . ."

1170   TRANSLATION AVAILABLE

Start your speech by speaking in a foreign language for a few minutes and then say, "At the conclusion of my speech a translation will be available for any of you who don't happen to speak (Chinese)."

1171   APPEAR "RELAXED"

Dab your forehead as if you were perspiring profusely and then remark: "The most important thing about public speaking is to be completely relaxed."

1172   SPEAKER DEFENDING HIMSELF

"I'm not asking you to like my speech, folks—but I think I ought to tell you that I'm a veteran with a wife and four small kids to support."

1173   SALUTING AUDIENCE-REASON FOR

Salute your audience and quip, "I always salute those who are about to have their courage tested."

1174   LAUNCHING AT JOKE ABOUT TO BE TOLD

Open with a big hearty laugh and then say, "Excuse me—I just couldn't help myself but I just remembered the joke I'm about to tell you."

1175   WARNING—ALL ON CANDID CAMERA

"Don't be upset, friends, but I thought I should warn you—you are all on Candid Camera."

1176   SPEAKERS APPRECIATIONS

"I am deeply appreciative of the fact that you turned down Bob Hope and insisted that *I* be your speaker tonight."

1177   LOCKED DOORS AND EXITS

"Will the ushers please lock all the doors and exits."

1178   SPEAKING THE TRUTH

"Ladies and gentlemen, unaccustomed as I am to public speaking—and in a few minutes you'll all agree on how true that is."

1179   SPEEDING SPEECH UP

Begin your speech by talking as rapidly as possible and then remark, "We're a little late today, folks, so I'll have to hurry things up a bit."

1180   YAWNING OPENER

Open with a big yawn and quip, "I'm sorry, friends, but I've heard this speech before."

1181   SPEECH FOR TONIGHT

"I have a very funny, entertaining speech—but that's not the one I'm giving tonight."

1182   VOICE—TUNING UP

Hum loudly for a few seconds and then announce, "I always tune my voice up before I start a speech."

1183 PUBLIC SPEAKING EXPERT—COMMENTS OF

"I want you people to know that I turned my speech over to a public speaking expert for his comments before I came here tonight and despite his remarks I'm going ahead with my speech."

1184 V FOR VICTORY

Hold up your hand with your fingers in the V for Victory position and announce. "It worked for Winston Churchill—maybe it will help me tonight."

1185 APOLOGIZING

"First I want to apologize for being able to make it here tonight . . ."

1186 NERVOUS TONIGHT

Jerk your head from side to side, or tremble violently, and quip. "If I seem nervous tonight, folks, it's only because—I am!"

1187 WHEN TO START SLEEPING

"Will the gentleman in the rear who is sleeping, at least please wait until I start my speech."

1188 SILENT PRAYER FOR SPEAKER

Bow your head and quip, "There will now be one minute of silent prayer for the speaker."

1189 SPEAKER ALMOST LATE—REASON FOR

"I was almost late because I hadn't quite finished memorizing my ad-lib speech for tonight."

1190 MY VOICE—SOUND OF

Hold your hands over your ears and quip, "I hope you don't mind but, frankly, I can't stand the sound of my voice."

1191 STATIONARY ARMS

Fold your arms and remark, "You will notice that not once during my speech will my arms leave my shoulders."

1192 GETTING PLEASURE OUT OF TALKING—REASON FOR

"It gives me a great deal of pleasure to have this opportunity to talk to you. Perhaps you are curious to know why this should give me so much pleasure. The answer is simple. You see, I am easily entertained. All I need is someone to listen to me!"

1193 SUBJECT OF TALK—TWO MINUTES

"Good evening, ladies and gentlemen. Before I arrived tonight I asked my wife what I should talk about and she said, 'About two minutes.' "

1194 AD-LIB REMARKS—PREPARATION OF

"I hope you enjoy my ad-lib remarks tonight. I spent two weeks preparing them."

1195 MIRACLE—IN OLD DAYS, NOWADAYS

"In the old days of the Bible it was considered a miracle if an ass spoke. Now it happens all the time."

1196 A MAN OF FEW WORDS

"If my speech appears short and to the point, it is because I have always been a strong believer in the guiding principle that it is best to be a man of few words. A man of few words doesn't have so many to take back."

1197 DOUBLE PARKED VOLKSWAGON

"Will the gentleman in the audience who double parked his Volkswagon on top of the Cadillac please remove it at once."

1198 REMARKS ABOUT SPEECH

"I hope you'll say about my speech tonight what they wrote on a tombstone in Arizona, 'Here lies Jack Williams. He done his damndest.' "

1199   WHAT IS AN ANECDOTE?

"I was going to begin my speech with an anecdote until I happened to read a definition of an anecdote: 'A joke that has seen better days.' "

ABSENTMINDEDNESS

2001   ABSENTMINDED MAN

One of the most absentminded men was Paul Painleve—thrice Premier of France. It is said that he would take a taxi home when his car was waiting for him. And when the taxi driver asked for his address, he would often give his telephone number. One time, when he was expecting a visitor, he pinned a note on his own door: "Painleve will return in fifteen minutes." On returning he saw his own note and sat down on the step to wait for himself.

ACTORS

2002   HANDLING DISTURBANCE IN AUDIENCE

The actor John Kemble was once performing in a play when time and time again he was interrupted by the squalling of a child in the audience. At length, becoming angered by this, he walked solemnly to the front of the stage and addressing the audience, he announced in tragic tones: "Ladies and gentlemen, unless the play is stopped, the child cannot possibly go on."

2003   IMITATION OF AN OPERA STAR

At a dinner in Hollywood many years ago Charlie Chaplin entertained the guests by imitating a wide variety of people they knew. At one point he began to sing an aria from an Italian Opera and he sang it beautifully. "Charlie," someone exclaimed, "I never knew you could sing so superbly." "Why, I can't sing at all," replied Chaplin, "I was only imitating Caruso."

2004   DT'S END, HOLLYWOOD BEGINS

W. C. Fields was one of Hollywood's most fervent drinkers. When asked by an interviewer if he had ever suffered from DTs, Field replied, "I can't tell, because I have never been able to discover where the DTs end and Hollywood begins."

ADVICE

2005   PRAISE WANTED

When a man seeks your advice he generally wants your praise.

Lord Chesterfield

2006   ADVICE TO MOVIE PRODUCER

The number of people giving unsolicited advice to the President reminded Rep. Sidney Yates (D. Ill.) of a story George Jessel tells about his first meeting with a movie producer. "I told him how he could do things so much better," Jessel says, "that he thanked me for the advice. The he boarded his yacht and I took the subway home."

2007   DIFFERENCE BETWEEN GIVING AND TAKING ADVICE

"Advice is like castor oil, easy enough to give but very hard to take."

Josh Billings

AMERICA

2008   AMERICA, DISCOVERY HUSHED UP

America had often been discovered before Columbus—but it had always been hushed up.

Oscar Wilde

2009   FINDING AMERICA—MISSING IT

It was wonderful to find America, but it would have been more wonderful to miss it.

Mark Twain

ANIMALS AND LIFE

2010   MEN VERSUS DOGS

The more I see of men, the more I like dogs.   *Madame de Stael*

2011   A DOG AND A MAN

If you pick up a starving dog and make him prosperous, he will not bite you. This is the principal difference between a dog and a man.   *Mark Twain*

2012   COOPERATION BETWEEN WILD CREATURES

There is some cooperation between wild creatures; the stork and the wolf usually work the same neighborhood.   *Robert Quillen*

2013   DIFFERENCE BETWEEN MAN AND ANIMAL

Man is the only animal that laughs and weeps; for he is the only animal that is struck with the difference between what things are, and what they ought to be.
                                                                   Hazlitt

AUDACITY

2014   SHORTENING INTERVIEWS

An elderly Boston newspaperman interviewing playwright John Patrick apologized for cutting the interview short. He had to cover a show at the planetarium, he explained. "They're reproducing the sky exactly as it was the night Christ was born."

"Over Bethlehem?" Patrick asked.

"Of course not," the reporter answered indignantly, "Over Boston."
                                                                   Leonard Lyons

2015   CONDEMNED MAN PLEADING FOR MERCY

He reminds me of the man who murdered both his parents, and then, when

sentence was about to be pronounced, pleaded for mercy on the grounds that he
was an orphan.   *Abraham Lincoln*

2016   DRAWING IN A COMPETITION—A REPLY TO THE COMPANY

When he was at the height of his fame, Charles Dana Gibson was invited by an
automobile company to submit a drawing in a competition. In writing to the artist,
the company specified that the drawing would win a cash prize if accepted, but then
audaciously stated that if it was rejected it would become the property of the company. Gibson's eminently fair reply was: "I am running a competition for automobiles. Kindly submit one of yours. If acceptable, it wins an award. If rejected, it
becomes my property."

2017   REPLIES TO BORROWERS

Mark Twain was an inveterate book borrower. One day he asked a neighbor for
a loan of a certain book. The neighbor said, "Yes, but it is my rule that any volume
taken from my library must be read on the premises."

Several weeks later the same neighbor waited to borrow the Twain lawn mower.
"Certainly you may use it," said Twain. "But I have made a rule that any lawn
mower of mine that is borrowed must be used on my own lawn."

AUTOMOBILES

2018   INVENTION OF THE WHEEL

What a lucky thing the wheel was invented before the automobile; otherwise,
can you imagine the awful screeching?   *Samuel Hoffenstein*

2019   SUGGESTED SAFE DRIVING SLOGAN

Asked for a slogan to encourage safe driving over a big holiday weekend,
George Gobel suggested: "Ladies and gentlemen, this is a holiday weekend. The
National Safety Council estimates that 354 people will be killed. So far, only 172
have been killed. Some of you folks aren't trying!"

BOOKS

2020   REASON FOR NOT READING BOOKS

I've given up reading books; I find it takes my mind off myself.   *Oscar Levant*

2021   FAVORITE BOOKS

For people who like that kind of a book, that is the kind of book they will like.
Abraham Lincoln

CHILDREN

2022   ADVANTAGES OF ADAM AND EVE

Adam and Eve had many advantages, but the principle one was that they escaped teething.   *Mark Twain*

2023   MEN—GREAT CHILDREN

Men, in general, are but great children.   *Napoleon*

CRITICISM

2024   HOW TO AVOID CRITICISM

To avoid criticism, do nothing, say nothing, be nothing.   *Elbert Hubbard*

2025   THE MAKING OF LITERARY CRITICS

Nature, when she invented, manufactured, and patented her authors, contrived to make critics out of the chips that were left.   *Oliver Wendell Holmes*

2026 PARTS OF A MANUSCRIPT

Your manuscript is both good and original, but the part that is good is not original, and the part that is original is not good.   *Dr. Samuel Johnson*

2027 OMISSION OF A STATUE IN HONOR OF CRITICS

Pay no attention to what the critics say. There has never been a statue set up in honor of a critic.   *Jean Sibelius*

DEBTS

2028 ATTACHMENTS ON A DEBTOR

If it isn't the sheriff, it's the finance company. I've got more attachments on me than a vacuum cleaner.   *John Barrymore*

2029 SHORTNESS OF A MONTH

You never realize how short a month is until you pay alimony.   *John Barrymore*

2030 MORTGAGE ON A HOUSE

The house was more covered with mortgages than with paint.   *George Ade*

DIETING AND NOT

2031 A SOLUTION TO THE WEIGHT PROBLEM

Jackie Gleason claims he's found the solution to his weight problem; he eats as much as he pleases and he drinks as much as he pleases. He just doesn't swallow.

2032 MAGNIFICENT PHYSIQUE

He must have had a magnificent build before his stomach went in for a career of its own.   *Margaret Halsey*

2033   A GIFT OF DELICIOUS FLOWERS

Pierre Salinger recalls a day when George Reedy, then the two-hundred-pound Press Secretary at the White House, was ordered to a hospital to go on a strict diet and lose some weight. When his office staff sent him a big basket of flowers, Reedy acknowledged the gift with this wire: "Thank you for the flowers. They were delicious."

2034   BREAKFAST BEFORE NINE IN THE MORNING

The giraffe must get up at six in the morning if it wants to have its breakfast in its stomach by nine.   *Samuel Butler*

2035   SECRET COOKING LESSONS

Several years after she had married Charlie MacArthur, great star Helen Hayes announced to him and their young son James that she had secretly been taking cooking lessons, and proposed to cook dinner for them that very evening. "If I spoil it," she ordered, "I don't want to hear a word from either of you. We'll just get up from the table, without comment, and go to a restaurant for dinner."

A short time later, she entered the dining room, bearing aloft the first steak she ever had cooked. Mr. MacArchur and son Jamie were sitting in silence at the table —with their hats and coats on.

2036   INEDIBLE CANNED GOODS—TENNIS BALLS

When Joseph E. Davies became Ambassador to Russia, he and Mrs. Davies took with them tons of canned stuff. Their Russian cook was puzzled by one can, and he finally confessed to Mrs. Davies that no matter how long he cooked the contents, no matter how many sweets he added, it was still inedible. Investigation revealed that the can had contained three tennis balls.

DISHONESTY

2037   A THOUGHT ABOUT LYING

I do not mind lying, but I hate inaccuracy.   *Samuel Butler*

2038   FOOLING PEOPLE

You can fool some of the people all of the time, and all of the people some of the time, but you cannot fool all of the people all of the time.   *Abraham Lincoln*

2039   IDEAS AS TO PLAGIARISM

Nicholas Murray Butler and Professor Brander Matthews of Columbia University were having a conversation, and Prof. Matthews was giving his ideas as to plagiarism, from an article of his own on that subject.

"In the case of the first man to use an anecdote," he said, "there is originality; in the case of the second there is plagiarism; with the third, it is lack of originality; and with the fourth it is drawing from a common stock."

"Yes," broke in President Butler, "and in the case of the fifth, it is research."

DOCTORS

2040   "DOCTORS" COMING TO THE AID

Humorist Stephen Leacock had a long string of college degrees, and Canadian associates usually addressed him as "Doctor." The purser of an Atlantic liner, who had heard him thus referred to for three days, stepped up to him one evening and said, "Doctor, could I prevail upon you to examine the star of last year's Ziegfeld Follies? She slipped on the promenade deck and I'm afraid she has sprained her hip." Leacock reported ruefully later, "I rushed there like a startled gazelle, but alas! Two doctors divinity had beaten me to it."

2041   MISTAKES OF DOCTORS AND ARCHITECTS

The physician can bury his mistakes, but the architect can only advise his clients to plant vines.
                                                                      Frank Lloyd Wright

2042   DOCTOR'S DIAGNOSIS OF A PAINTING

Samuel F. B. Morse, who was a painter before he invented the telegraph, once asked a physician friend to look at his painting of a man in death agony. "Well," Morse inquired after the doctor had scrutinized it carefully, "What is your opinion?"

"Malaria," said the doctor.

DRAMA

2043   COMMENT ON THE RESPONSE OF AN AUDIENCE

Oscar Wilde arrived at his club one evening, after witnessing a first production of a play that was a complete failure.

"Oscar, how did your play go tonight?" said a friend.

"Oh," was the lofty response, "the play was a great success but the audience was a failure.

2044   OPENING NIGHT OF PLAY

On the opening night of "The Solid Gold Cadillac," while Kaufman was brooding more deeply than usual awaiting the outcome, he was joined at his home by a friend. After trying vainly to break through the pessimism the friend said, "Nice day."

Responded Mr. Kaufman: "It was a nice day when they burned Joan of Arc."

DRINKING

2045   DIAGNOSIS: INTOXICATION

When you find you can't stand the terrible crashing of snowflakes as they hit the ground, you've had enough.

Gerald Barzan

2046   NOISE OF BROMO-SELTZER

W. C. Fields was suffering from one of his daily hangovers. "May I fix you a Bromo-Seltzer?" suggested the waiter. Roared Fields: "Ye gods, no! I couldn't stand the noise."

2047   THE FOOLISHNESS OF DRINKING

Drinking makes such fools of people, and people are such fools to begin with, that it's compounding a felony.

Robert Benchley

2048   BENEFITS OF DRINKING WATER

Drinking water neither makes a man sick, nor in debt, nor his wife a widow.
John Neale

2049   DIFFERENCE BETWEEN GREEK DRINK AND EARTHQUAKE

Some years ago, Representative Olin Teague of Texas visited Greece. At an embassy party he was introduced to the popular Greek drink, ouzo. After the first glass he noticed the furniture moving around. "This is a powerful drink," he said to the ambassador.

"Not particularly," the ambassador replied. "This happens to be an earthquake."

2050   OUT OF WET CLOTHES, INTO A DRY MARTINI

Alexander Woollcott arrived at a friend's home one day during a severe rain storm and said, "I want to slip out of these wet clothes and into a dry martini."

EXERCISE

2051   ACTING OUT EXERCISE

I get my exercise acting as a pallbearer to my friends who do exercise.
Chauncey Depew

2052   JACKIE GLEASON'S EYELIDS—UP, DOWN, ONE AT A TIME

"Who says I don't do my exercises regularly in the mornings?" demands an indignant Jackie Gleason. "Immediately after awakening, I always say sternly to myself, 'Ready, now. Up. Down. Up. Down.' And after three strenuous minutes I tell myself, 'Okay, boy. Now we'll try the other eyelid.' "

FRIENDSHIP

2053 MISTAKEN FRIENDSHIP

Speaking of a mutual acquaintance, a friend said to Voltaire, "It is good of you to say such pleasant things of him when he says such spiteful ones of you."

"Perhaps," responded Voltaire, "we are both mistaken."

2054 A NOTHING FRIENDSHIP

Bing Crosby had this to say about a certain friend of his. "There's nothing in the world I wouldn't do for that guy, and there's nothing he wouldn't do for me— we spend our lives doing nothing for each other."

2055 LOYAL FRIENDSHIP

The holy passion of friendship is of so sweet and steady and loyal and enduring a nature that it will last through a whole lifetime, if not asked to lend money.

Mark Twain

FRUSTRATION

2056 KICKING A ROSE BUSH

Gene Fowler once caught the irascible Fields violently kicking a rose bush in his garden. "Bloom, damn you," Fields was muttering.

2057 CENTER OF ATTENTION

It was one of his own sons who so aptly characterized Theodore Roosevelt, saying, "Father always had to be the center of attention. When he went to a wedding, he wanted to be the bridegroom; and when he went to a funeral, he wanted to be the corpse."

2058 WORRIED EXPLORER

Two days before Christopher Columbus discovered land, he stood on the deck, very worried and confused. One of the crew finally said to him, "It's a shame that we wander on the sea this way, not knowing where anything is."

Replied Columbus, "I know where everything is. What worries me is, where are we?"

GAMBLING

2059   RACE HORSE TIP

Comedian Joe E. Lewis was thanking a friend for a race tip. "You said it was a great horse and it was," he said. "It took eleven other horses to beat that horse."

2060   MONEY IN THE RACES

The only man who makes money following the races is the one who does so with a broom and shovel.

Elbert Hubbard

2061   A WAY TO BET

It may be that the race is not always to the swift, nor the battle to the strong— but that's the way to bet.

Damon Runyon

2062   GAMBLING BUSINESS

The gambling known as business looks with austere disfavor upon the business known as gambling.

Ambrose Bierce

2063   HORSE'S NEEDS

Jimmy Durante bet on a horse at Santa Anita and the nag lost by inches. "What that horse needed." bragged an ex-jockey, "was my riding."

"What he needed," corrected Durante, "was my nose."

GOVERNMENT

2064   **WATCHING GOVERNMENT AND REPORTING FACTS**

I don't make jokes. I just watch the government and report the facts.

Will Rogers

2065   **A GOVERNMENT POLICY MAKER**

During World War I, Will Rogers had a suggestion for getting rid of the German submarine menace: "All we have to do is heat the Atlantic up to 212°F. Then the subs will have to surface, and we can pick them off one by one. Now, somebody's going to want to know how to warm up that ocean. Well, I'm not going to worry about that. That is a matter of detail, and I'm a policy maker."

2066   **PREFERENCE FOR NEWSPAPERS RATHER THAN GOVERNMENT**

Were it left to me to decide whether we should have a government without newspapers or newspapers without government, I should not hesitate a moment to prefer the latter.   *Thomas Jefferson*

2067   **REVOLUTIONS AND TRIFLES**

Revolutions are not about trifles, but spring from trifles.   *Aristotle*

2068   **MY COUNTRY—MY MOTHER**

"My country, right or wrong" is like saying, "My mother, drunk or sober."

Gilbert Keith Chesterton

HARD TIMES

2069   **CONTENTS OF A CIGARBOX**

Mark Twain was once a young and struggling newspaper writer in San Francisco and one day a lady of his acquaintance saw him with a cigarbox under his arm looking in a shop window. "Why Mr. Clemens," she exclaimed, "I always see you with a cigarbox under your arm. I am afraid you are smoking too much." "It isn't that," said Twain. "I'm moving again."

2070   FEELINGS OF DEFEAT

After he was defeated for the Presidency, Thomas E. Dewey said the best analogy of his feelings the day after—when he saw defeat snatched from the jaws of victory—was of the mourner who had passed out from too much drinking at a wake and was laid in a spare coffin in the funeral parlor to sleep it off. When he came to and realized where he was, he asked himself, "If I'm alive, why am I in this coffin? And if I'm dead, why do I have to go to the bathroom?"

2071   UNPAVED STREETS

On the Arthur Godfrey program, Sam Levenson was talking about his family. "My folks were immigrants," he said, "and they fell under the spell of the American legend that the streets of America were paved with gold. When Pop got here though, he found out three things: (1) The streets were not paved with gold; (2) the streets were not even paved and, (3) he was supposed to do the paving."

2072   DEFINITION OF ADVERSITY

Adversity is the state in which a man most easily becomes acquainted with himself, being especially free from admirers then.   *Samuel Johnson*

IDEALISM

2073   INCREASING IDEALISM

Idealism increases in direct proportion to one's distance from the problem.
                                                                    John Galsworthy

2074   HOW TO GRATIFY OR ASTONISH PEOPLE

Always do right. That will gratify some of the people, and astonish the rest.
                                                                    Mark Twain

2075   THINGS TO DO AND NOT TO DO

There is an old saying in Puerto Rico that a man must do three things during life—plant trees, write books and have sons. I wish they would plant more trees and write more books.

Louis Munoz Marin

KNOWLEDGE

2076   THE IGNORANT OR KNOWLEDGABLE ONE

When I was a boy of 14, my father was so ignorant I could hardly stand to have the old man around. But when I got to be 21, I was astonished at how much the old man had learned in seven years.

Mark Twain

2077   QUALITY OF MAN

I think there is only one quality worse than hardness of heart and that is softness of head.

Theodore Roosevelt

2078   WISDOM OUT OF AN EXPERIENCE

Mark Twain once observed safely, "One should be careful to get out of an experience only the wisdom that is in it—and stop there; lest we be like the cat that sits down on the hot stove lid. She will never sit down on a hot stove lid again—and that's well; but also she will never sit down on a cold one any more."

2079   RECRUIT GIVING MORE THAN NECESSARY

On occasion we all tend to give more information than is asked for. General Earle G. Wheeler, Army Chief of Staff, had this story to tell about a young recruit he happened to witness being inducted. The young man was being questioned by a sergeant: "Did you go to grammar school?"

"Oh, yes sir," the recruit quickly answered. "I also went through high school, graduated from Knox College, and took graduate study at Michigan and Harvard, where I got my phD.

The sergeant picked up a rubber stamp, inked it and then stamped the form 'Literate.' "

2080   LEARNING FROM HISTORY

We learn from history that we do not learn from history.

Georg Wilhelm Friedrich

2081   IGNORANCE OR KNOWLEDGE

I would rather have my ignorance than another man's knowledge, because I have so much of it.

Mark Twain

LAWYERS

2082   DEAD OR ALIVE YOU NEED A LAWYER

You cannot live without lawyers, and certainly you cannot die without them.

Joseph Choate

2083   TALKING WITHOUT THINKING

At one time Sir Henry Irving was a witness in a case of street robbery. The thief's lawyer screamed at the distinguished actor: "At what hour did the theft happen?"

"Well, I-I-think-" began Sir Henry.

The lawyer interrupted with, "It isn't what you *think* that we want to know."

"You don't want to know what I think?" the actor asked.

The lawyer snapped, "I do not!"

"Well, then," Sir Henry replied, "I might as well leave the witness box. I cannot talk without thinking. I'm not a lawyer."

LIFE AT HOME AND AWAY

2084   GOING HOME

Home is the place where, when you have to go there, they have to take you in.

Robert Frost

2085   HOTEL ROOM WALLS

I wish someone would tell me why hotel room walls are so thin when you sleep and so thick when you listen.

Arthur Godfrey

2086 REASON FOR LEAVING HIS BED BEHIND

I rise from bed the first thing in the morning not because I am dissatisfied with it, but because I cannot carry it with me during the day.   *Edgar Wilson Nye*

LOVE

2087 EMOTION AND EXPENSES

Love is an ocean of emotions, entirely surrounded by expenses.   *Lord DeWar*

2088 REASONS WHY LOVERS NEVER TIRE OF ONE ANOTHER

The reasons why lovers and their mistresses never tire of being together is that they are always talking of themselves.   *La Rochefoucauld*

2089 LOVE AT FIRST SIGHT

Adam invented love at first sight, one of the greatest labor saving devices the world ever saw.   *Josh Billings*

2090 COST OF FREE LOVE

After all, doesn't free love cost the most?   *Tom Masson*

LUCK

2091 LUCK AND HARD WORK

J. J. Lerner, owner of the stores bearing his name, met an admirer of his playwright son, Alan Jay, who authored such delights as *Brigadoon* and *Camelot*. "Isn't it wonderful how lucky your boy is?" said the man.

"Yes," replied Lerner, "isn't it wonderful? The harder he works, the luckier he gets."

2092   BELIEVING IN LUCK

Jean Cocteau, asked if he believed in luck, replied, "Certainly, how else do you explain the success of those you don't like?"

MAN AND LIFE

2093   MAN'S REPUTATION AND HIS CHARACTER

Many a man's reputation would not know his character if they met on the street.
Elbert Hubbard

2094   MASTERPIECE—WHO SAYS SO?

Man is Creation's masterpiece; but who says so?—Man.   *Elbert Hubbard*

2095   NOT NECESSARY TO FOOL PEOPLE

You can't fool all of the people all of the time—but it isn't necessary!
Will Rogers

2096   HEALTHY, WEALTHY, AND DEAD

Early to rise and early to bed makes a male healthy and wealthy and dead.
James Thurber

2097   SOLUTION TO A HUMAN PROBLEM

There is always an easy solution to every human problem—neat, plausible and wrong.   *H. L. Mencken*

2098   MAN WHO BLUSHES

Man is the only animal that blushes—or needs to.   *Mark Twain*

2099   HAD NOAH MISSED THE BOAT

When you think of the condition of the world today, you sometimes wish that Noah had missed the boat.   *Bishop Fulton J. Sheen*

**2100   WHAT'S THE MATTER WITH THE BOYS?—WHAT'S THE MATTER
         WITH THE WHOLE WORLD?**

One of Abraham Lincoln's neighbors in Springfield, Ill. told the following:
One day, arrested by the cries of children, I looked out the door and saw Mr.
Lincoln stalking by with two of his boys. Both of them were weeping out loud.
"What's the matter with the boys, Mr. Lincoln?" I asked.
The future president looked at me, smiled, and answered:
"Just what's the matter with the whole world. I've got three walnuts and each
wants two."

2101   A DEGENERATE NOBLEMAN AND A TURNIP

A degenerate nobleman, or one that is proud of his birth, is like a turnip; there
is nothing good of him but that which is underground.   *Samuel Butler*

2102   BAD SINGER

Swans sing before they die—
    'twere no bad thing
Should certain persons die before they sing.   *Coleridge*

MARRIAGE

2103   SYSTEM FOR PRESERVING DOMESTIC WELL-BEING AND TRANQUILLITY

Jack Cominsky of the *Saturday Review* once boasted of a system he had invented
to preserve domestic well-being and tranquillity. "The day we were married, fifteen
years ago," he said, "we decided that really important decisions were to be left to
me. Small, everyday decisions that affected only the smooth running of the house
were left entirely to my wife."
"How has your system worked out?" asked a friend.
"Perfectly," said Cominsky. "There hasn't been a single hitch in the entire
fifteen years. "Of course," he added thoughtfully, "no really important decision has
come up yet."

2104   EXASPERATING WIFE AND COOKING

There is one thing more exasperating than a wife who can cook and won't, and
that's a wife who can't cook and will.   *Robert Frost*

2105   INCOMPATIBILITY—THE SPICE OF LIFE

A little incompatibility is the spice of life, particularly if he has income and she is pattable.   *Ogden Nash*

2106   REASON FOR MATRIMONY

The reason for so much matrimony is patrimony.   *Ogden Nash*

2107   SUBJECT OF MARRIAGE

Marriage is the one subject on which all women agree and all men disagree.
                                                                              Oscar Wilde

2108   RESULTS OF FAMILIARITY

Familiarity breeds contempt—and children.   *Mark Twain*

2109   HOUSEWIFE—ALL BY MYSELF

The best way for a housewife to get a few minutes to herself at the end of the day is to start doing the dishes.   *Arthur Godfrey*

2110   MAN'S COMPLIMENT TO WIFE—HIGHEST AND LAST

When a man makes a woman his wife, it's the highest compliment he can pay her, and its usually the last.   *Helen Rowland*

2111   PHILOSOPHER'S ADVICE TO WIVES ABOUT HUBBY'S HOBBIES

Advice to wives from that sage old philosopher, Peter Lind Hayes: "Remember, girls, your hubby still gets a bang out of golf, hunting trips, and all-night poker. Show him you're thinking of him! Speak of them occasionally!"

2112   BEAUTIFUL WIFE—FOR WORDS, FOR ARGUMENTS

My wife was too beautiful for words, but not for arguments.   *John Barrymore*

2113   REASON ARCHEOLOGIST MAKES BEST HUSBAND

An archeologist is the best husband any woman can have. The older she gets the more he is interested in her.   *Agatha Christie*

2114   PETER AND CHRIST—ON FRIENDLY TERMS

Peter remained on friendly terms with Christ, not withstanding Christ's having healed his mother-in-law.   *Samuel Butler*

2115   THE SHOE THAT PINCHES

A citizen of ancient Rome sought to divorce his wife, and as a result was severly chastened by his friends, who asked: "Was she not chaste? Was she not fair?"

The Roman held out one of his shoes. "Is it not well made?" he said. "Is it not also new?" And when they had agreed that the shoe was both well made and new, the Roman said: "Yet none of you can tell where it pinches me."   *Plutarch*

2116   TWO THINGS TO REMEMBER

If you would have a happy family life, remember two things: In matters of principle, stand like a rock; in matters of taste, swim with the current.

Thomas Jefferson

MILLIONAIRES

2117   TWO WHOLE YEARS' INTEREST ON A DOLLAR

John D. Rockefeller borrowed a dime from his secretary one day to pay his bus fare home from his office. "Be sure to remind me of this transaction," he said.

"Oh, that's nothing, Mr. Rockefeller," the secretary replied.

"Nothing!" exclaimed Rockefeller. "Why, that's two whole years' interest on a dollar!"

2118   THAT BEING THE CASE—I'D PURCHASE TWO OF THEM

The famous Dallas department store, Neiman-Marcus, had a visit from the wife of a multimillionaire oil tycoon. She wanted a new fur coat, and owner Stanley Marcus waited on her in person. She inclined to a modest number that bore a price tag of exactly $32,000. Marcus told her, "We must warn everybody who picks out a coat of this particular fur that while it is very, very rare and uncommonly beautiful, it doesn't wear as well as, say, mink or sable, and may no longer look its best after two or three seasons. That being the case, I suppose you'll reconsider the purchase."

"On the contrary," said the customer promptly; "That being the case, I'd better have two of them!"

2119   DONATION FROM OLD MAN AND SON—MY SON HAS A RICH FATHER: MINE WAS POOR

A committee called on John Jacob Astor for a donation to some worthy charity. The old man took the subscription list, looked it over, and wrote out a check for $50. They had expected much more, and one of them ventured to say: "We did hope for more, Mr. Astor; your son gave us $100."

"Ah," said the old man, "my son has a rich father. Mine was poor."

2120   RARITY OF EGGS AND MILLIONAIRES

When Rubenstein, the famous millionaire, came to a small town in the Ukraine, the people poured out to greet him. He was led by the town officials with all ceremony to the local inn, where he ordered two eggs for breakfast. When he was finished, the inn's proprietor said the charge was 20 rubles. Rubenstein was both astonished and angered.

"Never," said he, "have I been charged so much for two eggs. Are eggs such a rarity around here?"

"No," said the innkeeper, " but millionaires are."

MONEY AND PRICES

2121   WHERE DID THE MONEY GO

Never ask of money spent
Where the spender thinks it went
Nobody was ever meant
To remember or invent
What he did with every cent.

Robert Frost

2122   HIGH COSTS AT CHURCH FUNCTIONS

While President, Abraham Lincoln attended a large church bazaar. Wanting to buy a bunch of violets, he gave the lady at the booth a twenty dollar bill. She made no attempt to return any change and gushed, "Oh, thank you, Mr. President."

At this, Lincoln reached down from great height and gently touched the lady on the wrist, saying, "And what do you call this?"

"Why Mr. President, that is my wrist. What did you think it was?"

Drawled Lincoln, "Well, I thought it might be your ankle. Everything is so high around here."

OLD AGE

2123 ADVICE OF OLD MEN

Old men are fond of giving good advice, to console themselves for being no longer in a position to give bad examples.   *La Rochefoucauld*

2124 WHISTLER IN HIS LATER YEARS

There is a pathetic note as well as the usual wry humor in the statement Whistler wrote in his later years:

"I'm lonesome. They are all dying. I have hardly a warm personal enemy left."

OPEN AND CLOSED MIND

2125 CHANGE OF OPINIONS

The foolish and the dead alone never change their opinions.

James Russell Lowell

2126 CRISIS IN INTEGRATION

In 1963, when Lyndon B. Johnson, as Vice President, spoke at the Tufts University commencement, he was asked by newsmen if he thought the great crisis in integration had caught the country by surprise. In reply, Johnson recalled a story told about Ralph Waldo Emerson and fellow transcendentalist Margaret Fuller. Emerson saw Miss Fuller walk into a tree. Helping her to her feet, he asked, "Didn't you see the tree?"

"I saw it," Miss Fuller replied. "I just didn't realize it."

2127   LIKE PARACHUTES

Minds are like parachutes—they only function when open.

Thos. Robert Dewar

OPTIMISM

2128   OPTIMISM IN A LUNATIC ASYLUM

The place where optimism most flourishes is the lunatic asylum!

Havelock Ellis

2129   LIFETIME SPENT ON WISHBONE

A man will sometimes devote all his life to the development of one part of his body—the wishbone.   *Robert Frost*

PATIENCE AND QUIET

2130   DEFENSE PRODUCTION PROGRESS—IT STILL TAKES NINE MONTHS

William S. Knudsen, questioned by a House Committee about the progress being made in defense production during World War II, finally said, "Gentlemen, it's like this. Despite our modern hospitals, anesthetics, obstetricians, psychiatrists and gynecologists—despite all the advances in research, medicine and science—it still takes nine months."

2131   A FEELING ABOUT BEING ALONE

In Genesis it says that it is not good for a man to be alone, but sometimes it is certainly a great relief.   *John Barrymore*

PESSIMISM

2132   WHAT IS A PESSIMIST

What is a pessimist?: A man who thinks everybody is as nasty as himself, and hates them for it.
George Bernard Shaw

2133   A BLESSED PERSON

Blessed is he who expects nothing, for he shall never be disappointed.
Alexander Pope

2134   DEFINITION OF A CYNIC

A cynic is a man who, when he smells flowers, looks around for a coffin.
H. L. Mencken

2135   NOT MISTAKE TO BELIEVE EVIL:

It is a sin to believe evil of others, but it is seldom a mistake.   *H. L. Mencken*

PLAIN PEOPLE

2136   DISCRIMINATION OF THE STORK

About the only thing we have left that actually discriminates in favor of the plain people is the stork.
Frank McKinney Hubbard

2137   AN EXPRESSION OF GOD'S LOVE

God must have loved plain people; he made so many of them.
Abraham Lincoln

POLITICS

2138 STEPPING INTO THE REPUBLICAN PLATFORM

Shortly after the massive Democratic victory in the presidential election of 1964, Vice-President Humphrey was spending a few days at the LBJ ranch in Texas. One day Johnson was showing Humphrey around the pastures when Humphrey suddenly stopped, lifted a foot gingerly, and called out, "Mr. President, I just stepped into the Republican platform."

2139 PICKING ON A PRESIDENT

They pick a President and then for four years they pick on him.

Adlai Stevenson

2140 GETTING RID OF GOVERNMENT BUREAUS

When President Truman announced he was getting rid of some unnecessary government bureaus, a woman wrote him that since she was building a new house and needed furniture, she would appreciate a few of the discarded bureaus. Truman replied that he had disposed of the bureaus, but that if she was interested, he had a second-hand, no-damned-good cabinet he'd like to get rid of.

2141 PRAYER FOR SENATORS OR COUNTRY

When Edward Everett Hale was Chaplain of the Senate, someone asked him, "Do you pray for the senators, Dr. Hale?" "No, I look at the Senators and pray for the country," he said.

2142 INCURABLE OFFICE SEEKER ON DEATH OF CITY OFFICIAL

An incurable office seeker, upon learning of the death of a city official, went quickly to Mayor Walker and asked, "Can't I take Shanahan's place?"
"I have no objection," said Walker, "if the undertaker hasn't."

2143 DISCUSSION OF SERMON WITH WIFE

On his return from church one Sunday, Calvin Coolidge was asked by his wife what the minister spoke about.

"Sin," said Coolidge.

"What did he say about it?" asked Mrs. Coolidge.

Replied Coolidge, "He was against it."

2144 FLATTENED AT THE POLES

At New York's Dutch Treat Club, the late Frank Crowninshield was once obliged to introduce a politician who had just been clobbered unmercifully in a bid for re-election to Congress. "Gentlemen," began Crowninshield in silky tones, "our next speaker bears a strong resemblance to the earth. You will recall that the earth is not a perfect spheroid, because it is flattened at the poles. That's precisely what happened to our next speaker."

2145 HATS FOR POLITICIANS

Every politician, suggested Carl Sandburg, should have three hats handy at all times: one for throwing into the ring, another for talking through, and a third for pulling rabbits out of if elected!

2146 PATRIOTIC POLITICIANS

The politicians were talking themselves red, white, and blue in the face.

Clare Booth Luce

2147 NEIGHBOR VOTING FOR REPUBLICANS

Franklin Delano Roosevelt enjoyed telling a story about meeting an old neighbor during his third term campaigh. "Who are you voting for this year?" Roosevelt inquired.

The man replied, "For the Republicans."

"How come?" Roosevelt asked. "Does the third term bother you?"

"Oh it isn't that at all, Franklin," replied the neighbor.

"It's just that, frankly, I voted Republican the first time you ran, I voted Republican the second time you ran, and I'm going to vote Republican again—because I never had it so good!"

2148 STATEMENT OF DEATH OF DISLIKED FRIEND

Voltaire, asked for a comforting statement on the death of a politician he disliked, wrote the following:

"I have just been informed that Monsieur—is dead. He was a sturdy patriot, a gifted writer, a loyal friend, and an affectionate husband and father—provided he is really dead."

2149 GOING TO CONGRESS, HEAVEN OR HELL

One of the Lincoln stories has it that, during his 1846 campaign for Congress, he attended a preaching service of Peter Cartwright. The Evangelist called on all who wished to go to Heaven to stand up. All rose but Lincoln. The Evangelist called for all to rise who did not want to go to Hell. "I am grieved," said Cartwright, "to see Abe Lincoln sitting back there unmoved by these appeals. If he doesn't want to go to Heaven and doesn't want to escape Hell, will he tell us where he does want to go?"

Lincoln got up slowly and said, "I'm going to Congress."

2150 NAME CHANGING IN POLITICS

At a meeting in the White House, Rep. Thomas O'Neill, Jr. of Massachusetts passed along to President Kennedy a Kennedy family joke which JFK enjoyed. In this tale, the youngest member of the clan, Sen. Edward M. Kennedy, appears in a probate court and asks to have his name changed.

"One of my brothers is President," the Senator tells the judge, "and another is Attorney General. I want to make it on my own. I don't want to have a name like Kennedy that is so well-known politically."

"I can understand that," the judge says. "What name do you want instead of Teddy Kennedy?"

"I'd like to keep Teddy," the Senator says, "and change my last name to Roosevelt."

2151 THE ART OF GOVERNMENT

Senator William Proxmire had the following story to tell while speaking before an audience in Chicago:

"In Milwaukee we haven't quite learned the art of government as you have learned it here in Chicago. You have a certain skill and a certain touch which we are working on, but we haven't quite achieved it yet. Just recently, I was shaking hands with some of my constituents and a fellow came up to me and said, "Proxmire, I have been for you from the beginning. All those times you ran for governor, I voted for you every time. I voted for you when you ran for the Senate. I have always voted for you."

I said, "Wonderful! What can I do for you?"

He said, "Well, Senator, there is something you can do for me. I am trying to get my citizenship."

2152 "OOMPAH-OOMPAH ON AN INDIAN RESERVATION

Then there was Walter Richard's story of the day during the 1948 campaign when Mr. Truman's train stopped at an Indian reservation and the President emerged to deliver a speech. "I am appalled," he said, "at the treatment of you noble redmen and women by the administrations previous to mine, particularly the

Republicans." He made a gesture as though he was chopping a Republican in the neck and continued: "As our train pulled in, I saw squaws washing clothes by the riverside, pummeling them on rocks, even as your ancestors did. I intend to see a Bendix installed in every teepee!"

The Indians broke into loud cries of "Oompah-oompah!"

The President broke into his broadest grin and soared to a climax.

"If re-elected, I intend to see that your noble chief drives a Cadillac as big as mine, and a new Pontiac shall stand before every teepee."

As he bowed, the Indians roared out their mightiest "Oompah" and their handsome chief came forward and placed a war bonnet on the President's head. Then he led the Great White Father to the corrals for another presentation, delivering the speech in the impeccable English of a Carlyle graduate. "The Indians of this reservation take great pleasure in presenting as a token of our esteem a silver-mounted saddle and our very best Indian pony." As the President prepared to mount the handsome animal, the Chief suddenly cried out, "Be careful, Mr. Truman. Don't step in the oompah!"

2153 LAST PRAYER IN OLD HOME

How much did Adlai Stevenson enjoy living in New York? Well, in 1964, he told a story in Washington—and with great relish, too—about a family about to move to Manhattan. The young daughter was saying her very last prayer in her old home. It went as follows: "Bless my daddy, bless my mommy, bless my brother Freddy. And now, dear Lord, I'll have to say goodbye to You. We are moving to New York. Amen."

POPULARITY

2154 SWOONING FANS OF STARS

Ed Wynn says there's only one difference between himself and Pat Boone: "We're both extremely popular," he explains, "but when my fans swoon, it takes them longer to get up."

2155 DISLIKED FIGURES IN SHOWBUSINESS

Bert Lahr and some friends were discussing one of the most disliked figures in show business. "I wish somebody would kidnap him." one of Mr. Unpopularity's enemies said.

"Who would they contact?" asked Lahr.

2156   TURNED UP NOSES

When you are down and out, something always turns up—and it's usually the noses of your friends.
Orson Welles

2157   SEEING IS BELIEVING

When I was a boy I was told that anybody could become President; I'm beginning to believe it.
Clarence Darrow

2158   BEING TALKED ABOUT

There is only one thing in the world worse than being talked about, and that is not being talked about.
Oscar Wilde

PRAYER AND RELIGION

2159   TEN COMMANDMENTS—ONLY TEN

Say what you will about the Ten Commandments, you must always come back to the pleasant fact that there are only ten of them.
H. L. Mencken

2160   PRAYING AND WORKING—GOD AND MAN

Pray as if everything depended on God, and work as if everything depended upon man.
Francis Cardinal Spellman

2161   CREATION OF A PARSON

Had God thought that sin would enter Eden, He would have created a parson also.
Laurence Stern

2162   WEARING MOURNING FOR FRIENDS

I do not believe that it will always be popular to wear mourning for friends, unless we feel a little doubtful about where they went.
Edgar Wilson Nye

2163   POWER OF THE JUDGE

A friend once joked with Lord Salisbury by stating that a bishop was a man of greater authority than he, a jurist. The friend said, "A judge can do no more than say, 'You be hanged.' A bishop has the power to say, 'You be damned.'" "That may be true," said Salisbury, "but when a judge says, 'You be hanged,' you are hanged!"

PUBLIC SPEAKING

2164   GOOD THING GOING FOR ADAM

What a good thing Adam had—when he said a good thing, he knew nobody had said it before.   *Mark Twain*

2165   HONEST IKE AND AN HONEST OLD COW: GIVING ALL THEY HAVE

General Dwight D. Eisenhower, awarding the Medal of Merit to a group of war correspondents at ceremonies in the National Press Club, said he regretted he was not enough of an orator to do justice to the medal's recipients.

"It reminds me of my boyhood days on a Kansas farm," Ike related. "An old farmer had a cow that we wanted to buy. We went over to visit him and asked about the cow's pedigree. The old farmer didn't know what pedigree meant, so we asked him about the cow's butterfat production. He told us that he hadn't any idea what it was. Finally, we asked him how many pounds of milk the cow produced each year.

"The farmer shook his head and said: 'I don't know. But she's an honest old cow and she'll give you all the milk she has!'

"Well," the General concluded, "I'm like the cow; I'll give you everything I have."

2166   HEYWOOD BROUN—INTRODUCING HIS REPLY

Heywood Broun was once introduced to a lecture audience by an old-fashioned local politician who sang his praises in broken-down cliches for a full twenty minutes. Broun finally arose, smiled and said, "Ladies and Gentlemen, now I know how a pancake feels when they pour syrup on it."

2167   PLAYING TO AN EMPTY HOUSE—DANNY KAYE

Once, when Danny Kaye was playing at a theatre in Japan, the lights suddenly went out. In the darkness, the earthquake conscious Japanese audience stirred and murmured. Without hesitating, Danny fled to the wings, snatched up two flashlights and went back on stage. "I knew I had to avert a panic," he says, "so, turning those flashlights on my face, I grimaced and sang and danced. Soon the rustling and the murmuring ceased. I flung myself into the act with new abandon. The panic is over, I thought, as I danced; I've probably saved hundreds of lives! Then the theatre lights came on. I stopped dancing and turned off the flashlights. Not a seat was occupied. For an hour, I'd been playing to an empty house."

2168 INTRODUCING THE AFTER-DINNER SPEAKER—REPLY BY SPEAKER

Joseph H. Choate and Chauncey Depew were invited to a dinner. Mr. Choate was to speak, and it fell to the lot of Mr. Depew to introduce him, which he did thus: "Gentlemen, permit me to introduce Ambassador Choate, America's most inveterate after-dinner speaker. All you need to do to get a speech out of Mr. Choate is to open his mouth, drop in a dinner, and up comes your speech."

Mr. Choate thanked the senator for his compliment, and then said, "Mr. Depew says if you open my mouth and drop in a dinner up will come a speech, but I warn you that if you open your mouths and drop in one of Senator Depew's speeches, up will come your dinners."

2169 TALKING PEOPLE—NOTHING TO SAY

People who have nothing to say are never at a loss in talking.   *Josh Billings*

2170 WORDS—DIFFERENCE BETWEEN

The difference between the right word and the almost right word is the difference between lightning and the lightning bug.   *Mark Twain*

2171 PRESENTING THE GUEST OF HONOR—WARNER'S BLANK ON DIPLOMAT'S NAME

Producer Jack Warner was to introduce a heroic diplomat at a dinner. He recited a memorized summary of the hero's accomplishments, reached the point where he was to present the guest of honor and drew a total blank on the diplomat's name. Warner solved it, to cheers, by gulping dramatically: "I'm too touched to go on," and sat down.

2172 TALKING MACHINE—INVENTION OF

A Toastmaster, in his introduction of Thomas Edison at a dinner, dwelt at length on the talking machine. Edison stood up, bowed, and said: I thank the gentleman for his kind remarks but I must insist upon a correction. *God* invented the talking machine. I only invented the first one that can be shut off."

2173   SOFT AND SWEET WORDS—REASON FOR

It's a good idea to keep your words soft and sweet, because you never know when you may have to eat them.

Dave Garroway

2174   BARTENDER IN PARIS—DETERMINING NATIONALITY OF CUSTOMERS

Former White House Press Secretary James Hagerty discovered a bartender in Paris who can determine the nationality of any customer after two double martinis. The bartender explained:

"Frenchman will want to make love; a Spaniard will dance; A German will boast; an Italian will sing; an Irishman will fight; and an American will want to make a speech."

2175   DENSE CROWD——GOVERNOR WARDEN OF CALIFORNIA ADDRESS TO

Chief Justice Warren, when Governor of California, began a political address thus: "Ladies and gentlemen, I'm pleased to see this dense crowd here tonight." A voice from the back shouted, "Don't be too pleased. We ain't all dense!"

2176   BLESSED PEOPLE WITH NOTHING TO SAY

Blessed are they who have nothing to say, and who cannot be persuaded to say it.

James Lowell

2177   WORDS AND REASON OF ORATOR

Here comes the orator, with his flood of words and his drop of reason.

Benjamin Franklin

2178   WORLD'S TALKING PEOPLE—HALF AND HALF

Half the world is composed of people who have something to say and can't, and the other half who have nothing to say and keep on saying it.   *Robert Frost*

2179   LONG SPEECHES AND TOO MANY OF THEM

George Bernard Shaw was once invited to speak at a dinner where there had been far too many speeches and they had been far too long for the patience of the audience. They waited expectantly for Mr. Shaw, who was last to speak. When the roar of the applause had subsided, "Ladies and gentlemen," he said, "The subject is not exhausted, but we are," and sat down.

2180   ONE-NIGHT STAND, HALF FILLED HOUSE

On a one-night stand in Flint, Michigan, Victor Borge was not daunted by the fact that the house was less than half filled. Looking out at the slim audience, he said, "Flint must be an extremely wealthy town I see that each of you bought two or three seats."

2181   CROWD AT POLITICAL SPEECH

One evening when Sir Winston Churchill was addressing a meeting in America, a woman cornered him and said in a heady, gushing voice: "Doesn't it thrill you, Mr. Churchill, to know that every time you make a speech the hall is packed to overflowing?"

"It is quite flattering," Mr. Churchill replied, "but whenever I feel this way I always remember that if instead of making a political speech I was being hanged, the crowd would be twice as big."

2182   GIFT FOR ORATORY

A reporter once said to George Bernard Shaw: "You have a marvelous gift for oratory. How did you develop it?"

Replied Shaw: "I learned to speak as men learn to skate or cycle, by doggedly making a fool of myself until I got used to it."

2183   CREDIT RECEIVED FOR SPEECH MAKING

William Lyon Phelps, the late Yale professor and popular lecturer, once said that he got credit for only one-fourth of the after-dinner speeches he made because ". . . every time I accept an invitation to speak, I really make four addresses. First, is the speech I prepared in advance. Which is usually pretty good. Then second is the speech I really make. And third is the speech I make on my way home, which is the best of all. Fourth is the speech the newspapers the next morning say I made, which bears no relation to any of the others."

2184   PAUSE IN IMPASSIONED SPEECH

Edmund Burke when delivering his impassioned speech against Warren Hastings suddenly stopped in the middle and slowly and impressively he raised his hand and pointed his finger at Mr. Hastings. As he stood there for a full minute with that dramatic pointing finger the audience held its breath. Then he continued.

Later, one of his associates remarked, "Mr. Burke, that was one of the most effective pauses I have ever seen. We in the audience simply held our breaths, wondering what you were going to say next."

"That," replied Mr. Burke, "is exactly the way I was feeling."

2185   LESS SPEAKING AND MORE THINKING

What this country needs is less public speaking and more private thinking.

Roscoe Drummond

2186   TOASTMASTER TO SPEAKER

The relationship of the toastmaster to speaker should be the same as that of the fan to the fan dancer. It should call attention to the subject without making any particular effort to cover it.

Adlai Stevenson

2187   TIME ALLOTMENT FOR SPEECHES

Woodrow Wilson was once asked how long he took to prepare a ten-minute speech. He said, "Two weeks."
"How long for an hour speech?"
"One week."

2188   CHAIRMAN'S REQUEST

A fraternal organization once asked George Jessel to play a benefit, and since it was in Brooklyn, his home territory, he agreed. A few days later, someone phoned him and suggested that he might also be able to line up Eddie Cantor. George said he would try and soon thereafter was able to report Cantor's acceptance.
"Ah, that's fine," beamed the chairman of the program committee.
"Now, just one thing more. If you can also get Bing Crosby, you won't have to come."

2189   ADVICE TO BANQUET SPEAKERS

Winston Churchill offers this advice to banquet speakers: "Say what you have to say and the first time you come to a sentence with a grammatical ending, sit down!"

2190   INTERRUPTION OF A SPEECH

On September 29, 1960, Harold Macmillan's speech before the United Nations was interrupted by the Russian Premier Nikita Khrushchev who took off his shoe and pounded the table with it. In the best tradition of British unflappability, Macmillan remarked calmly, "I'd like that translated, if I may."

2191   TWELVE-MINUTE SPEECH

When Vice-President Hubert Humphrey was asked to limit a commencement speech to twelve minutes, he said, "The last time I spoke for only twelve minutes was when I said hello to my mother."

2192   POLITICAL OPPONENT LOST HEAD

When hecklers once tossed a cabbage at William Howard Taft during a political speech, he paused and peered at it, and then said calmly: "Ladies and gentlemen, I see that one of my opponents has lost his head."

2193   EXPERIMENTS THAT DON'T WORK

When trying to develop a new storage battery, Thomas Edison experimented over 50,000 times before he succeeded. When his assistant commented on this, Edison exclaimed, "Results! Results? Why, man I have gotten a lot of results. I know fifty-thousand things that won't work."

2194   DISCIPLES AND APOSTLES

I have never heard anything about the *resolutions* of the disciples, but a great deal about the *Acts* of the Apostles.   *Horace Mann*

RETORTS

2195   ART OF MAKING ENEMIES

The artist, James McNeill Whistler, was well qualified to write a book on "The Gentle Art of Making Enemies." When he had finished painting a portrait of a London celebrity, he asked the man if he liked it.

"No, Mr. Whistler," was the reply; "I can't say that I do. You'll have to admit it's a bad work of art."

Whistler adjusted his monocle and looked at his sitter. Then he said: "Yes, but then you must admit you're a bad work of nature."

2196   HANDS OFF

It is said that Thomas Hart Benton one day intended to answer a speech of Calhoun's, but hearing that Calhoun was prostrated by illness and could not be present, he announced, "Benton will not speak today, for when God Almighty lays his hands on a man Benton takes his off."

2197   WHAT IS THE MOST BEAUTIFUL THING IN THE WORLD?

A woman once asked that great wit Chauncey Depew, "What is the most beautiful thing in the world?"

"Sleep", he replied.

"But, Mr. Depew," protested the lady, "I was sure you would agree with me that a beautiful woman is the most beautiful thing in the world."

"Of course, you are right," said Depew. "But next to a beautiful woman, sleep is the most beautiful thing in the world."

2198   A BRITISH COIN AND A NICKEL

When Coolidge was Governor of Massachusetts he was once host to a visiting Englishman of some prominence. The latter ostentatiously took a British coin from his pocket, saying, "My great, great grandfather was made a Lord by the King whose picture you see on this shilling?

Coolidge laconically produced a nickel. "My great, great grandfather," he said, "was made an angel by the Indian whose picture you see on this coin."

2199   THE WET CANVAS

Mark Twain once visited the artist Whistler in his studio and was looking over his pictures. He started to touch one canvas. "Oh," cried Whistler, "don't touch that! Don't you see it isn't dry yet?"

"I don't mind," replied Twain, "I have gloves on."

2200   AT THE OPERA WITH TALKING HOSTESS

Mark Twain was invited to be the guest of a box holder at the Metropolitan Opera House to hear "Aida," a favorite of the humorist. All through the performance, his hostess talked so much that no one could follow the music. As the last curtain descended, she turned to Twain and said effusively: "Dear Mr. Clemens, I hope you can join us again next Thursday evening. The opera is 'Tosca,' and I know you'll enjoy it."

"I'll be delighted," Mark rejoined, "I've never heard you in that."

2201   BRIDGE PARTNERS

Once George S. Kaufman, whose bridge was nearly as good as his dialogue, drew a particularly poor partner. After the first hand he asked her, "Do you mind if I inquire when you learned to play?" and before she could answer he added: "Oh, I know it was today. But I mean, what time today?"

2202   NEW CAR—OLD FRIEND

A fan offered Shelley Winters a new car. "Would you take it from a stranger?" exclaimed an associate.

"Anybody who offers me a new automobile," said Miss Winters, "automatically becomes an old friend."

2203   FEW WORDS AT CEREMONY

At the laying of a cornerstone, while President, Mr. Coolidge turned a spadeful of earth and then remained silent. The gathering expected him to speak. The master of ceremonies suggested that a few words would be fitting.

Mr. Coolidge looked over the upturned earth.

"That's a fine fishworm," said he.

2204   SILENCE AS REPARTEE

Silence is the unbearable repartee.   *Chesterton*

2205   CHAIRMAN COMPARED TO PARSLEY

Chairman Irving S. Olds of the U.S. Steel Corporation was presiding over a stockholders meeting when a woman arose and asked him, "Exactly what are the duties of a chairman: what do you do?"

Mr. Olds, without batting an eye, said "Madam, the chairman of the board is roughly equivalent to the parsley on a platter of fish."

2206   ORDERING LOBSTER—ALIVE AND DEAD

When Oscar Wilde and a friend both ordered lobster at lunch, the friend instructed the waiter, "Bring them quick!"

Said Wilde, "I'll have mine dead."

2207   BEARING OF FOOLS

Dorothy Parker was known for her wit. During one conversation with a particularly loquacious man, he announced to her, "I simply can't bear fools!"

Replied she, "Apparently your mother could."

2208   INTERVIEWER'S RETORT TO ACTOR

Beerbohm Tree was once trying to get a well-known actor back into his company. He invited the man to call and received him in his dressing room as he was making up.

"How much would you want to come back?" inquired Mr. Tree, busy with his paint pots. The actor named an exorbitant salary to which Tree replied as he went on making up: "Don't slam the door when you go out, will you?"

2209   DARWIN AND THE QUESTIONABLE BUG

The great naturalist, Charles Darwin, was once approached by two small boys of the family whose guest he was. They had caught a butterfly, a centipede, a beetle, and a grasshopper. Taking the centipede's body, the butterfly's wings, the beetle's head and the grasshopper's legs, they had glued them together to make an alarming and original insect.

"We caught this bug in the field," they said innocently. "What kind of a bug is it, Mr. Darwin?"

Darwin examined it with great solemnity. "Did you notice whether it hummed when you caught it, boys?" he asked gravely.

"Yes, sir," they answered, trying to conceal their mirth.

"Just as I thought," said Darwin. "It is a humbug."

2210   "LION HUNTERS"—INVITATION AND REPLY

The company of George Bernard Shaw has been much sought after by "lion hunters." One of these sent him an invitation as follows: "Lady so-and-so will be home Friday between four and six." Shaw sent the card back. At the bottom, he had written, "Mr. Bernard Shaw likewise."

2211   THE CHAMP AND THE SKINNY LITTLE RUNT

Murray Robinson tells about a time when John L. Sullivan, burly heavyweight champion, was downing a few beers in a Bowery saloon. A skinny little runt who had had a few too many staggered up to the champ and challenged him to a fight. John L. picked him three feet off the ground by the back of his coat, and grumbled, "Listen, you—if you hit me just once—and I find out about it . . ."

2212   RETORT TO HECKLER

During World War I, the immortal Will Rogers was delivering his monologue in the Ziegfeld Follies one evening when a hatchet-faced woman in the ninth row called out, "Why aren't you in the Army?" Rogers gave everybody in the audience time to turn around and look at his heckler, then drawled, "For the same reason, Madam, that you aren't in the Follies: physical disabilities."

2213   SECOND CLASS MEN

Thomas R. Marshall, (1854–1952) a noted lawyer and Vice President of the United States, once remarked:

"I come from Indiana, the home of more first-rate, second-class men than any state in the union."

2214   LIVING IN NEVADA OR HELL

Someone from Nevada once said, "With water to settle the dust, and congenial companions, Nevada would be all right." Ex-Senator Wade of Ohio retorted, "And with plenty of water and good society, Hell would not be a bad place to live in, either!"

2215   A MIND TO WRITE LIKE SHAKESPEARE

Wordsworth once said to Charles Lamb, "I believe I could write like Shakespeare, if I had a mind to try it." Replied Lamb, "Yes, nothing is wanting but the mind."

2216   BATTLE OF THE MARNE

Almost everybody thought that Marshal Joffre had won the first battle of the Marne during World War II, but some refused to agree. One day a newspaperman appealed to Joffre: "Will you tell me who did win the battle of the Marne?"

"I can't answer that," said the Marshal. "But I can tell you that if the battle of the Marne had been lost the blame would have been on me."

2217   STEPPING OFF THE STAGE

One day at rehearsal Sir Herbert Tree asked a youthful actor to "step back a little." The player did so. Tree eyed him critically and went on rehearsing. After a time he repeated his request: "A little further back." The youth obeyed. Surveying him, Tree went on with his work. Shortly afterwards he again asked him to step still further back.

"If I do," expostulated the youth, "I shall be right off the stage."

"Yes," said Tree, "that's right."

2218   ONLY GOD KNOWS THE ADDRESS

Ernest Hemingway, world traveller, once received a letter in Cuba addressed simply, "To Ernest Hemingway, God knows where!" The sender got a reply very promptly. "You were so right," scribbled Hemingway, "God knew!"

2219 EAGER-BEAVER BARBERS

Walter Pidgeon has a baffling answer for those eager-beaver barbers who hold up a mirror behind him after a haircut and ask, "Is this just the way you want it, sir?" Pidgeon takes a long hard look, then says, "Not quite. A little longer in the back, please."

2220 THE TRUCKMAN AND G.I. JOE

TV entertainer Harvey Stone recalls that when he was stationed at an army camp, he was assigned to work with fellow G.I. Joe Louis. One day the two men were driving when a truck sideswiped them. The driver hopped out, stuck his face in Joe's and obviously not recognizing the champ, bawled him out. After he had swaggered away, Harvey asked Joe why he had just sat there smiling instead of knocking the truckman flat.

"Well Harv," Joe drawled, "when somebody insulted Caruso, did he sing an aria for him?"

2221 ATTENTIVE TO HIS OWN APPLAUSE

Harpist Mildred Dilling tells this story about Harpo Marx, one of her pupils: "Harpo was playing a recital at my studio. When he left the stage, there was long applause, but he did not return for an encore or even for a bow. Later, I asked him why he had not responded to the tremendous applause."

"I couldn't," he replied. "I was out in front helping to keep it up."

2222 AMENDING A MOTION

During the meeting of the Constitutional Convention in Philadelphia, one of the members moved "that the standing army be restricted to 5000 men at any one time." George Washington, being the chairman, could not offer a motion, but he turned to another member and whispered: "Amend the motion to provide that no foreign enemy shall invade the United States at any time with more than 3000 troops."

2223 JOB OF AN UMPIRE

As President Truman tells it, he had very weak eyes as a boy and couldn't see well enough to play baseball. "Since I couldn't see the ball, they gave me a special job," he says.

"What was that, Mr. President?" somebody usually asks, "Cheerleader?"

"No," he replies, "Umpire."

2224   HAUNTING TUNE

Samuel Foote once asked a man why he forever sang one tune.

"Because it haunts me," replied the other.

"No wonder," Foote replied. "You continually murder it."

2225   WHISTLER'S FRENCH POODLE AND MACKENZIE'S FRONT DOOR

Whistler had a French poodle of which he was extravagantly fond. The poodle was seized with an infection of the throat, and Whistler had the audacity to send for the great throat specialist Sir Morell Mackenzie. Sir Morell, when he saw that he had been called in to treat a dog, didn't like it much, it was plain. But he said nothing. He prescribed, pocketed a big fee, and drove away. The next day he sent post-haste for Whistler, and Whistler, thinking he was summoned on some matter connected with his beloved dog, dropped his work and rushed like the wind to Mackenzie's. On his arrival Sir Morell said gravely: "How do you do, Mr. Whistler? I wanted to see you about having my front door painted."

2226   MODEL T FORD TOWN CAR

Invited to spend the weekend at Alexander Woollcott's house in Vermont, Harpo Marx arrived in a dilapidated Model T Ford with shredded side curtains and flapping fenders.

Staring down at the spectacle, Woollcott demanded, "What in the world is that?"

"Oh," replied Harpo loftily, "this is my town car."

"What town," demanded his outraged host, "Pompeii?"

2227   INTERVIEW WITH NOTHING TO SAY

When Heywood Broun was a cub reporter he once had to interview Senator Smoot for the *N.Y. World*. When Broun arrived the Senator from Utah announced, "I have nothing to say."

"I know," replied the young reporter, "now let's get down to the interview."

2228   DELAY IN BECOMING MEMBER

Arthur Godfrey was explaining why he had hesitated so long before becoming a member of a certain organization. "All the mail I got was on stationery marked 'From the desk of Walter Cronkite,' and I just never correspond with furniture."

2229   CONCERNING HEALTH

George Bernard Shaw, asked if he was well: "At my age, young man, you are either well or dead."

2230   GETTING TO KNOW YOU

When he was in America a number of years ago, Wu Ting Fang, the great Chinese diplomat, met an American woman at a reception. She did not know who he was, and she asked him sweetly:

"What 'nese' are you—Japanese, Javanese, or Chinese?"

"I am Chinese," replied Dr. Wu; and then he continued: "What 'kee' are you—monkey, donkey or yankee?"

2231   REACTION TO ELEGY

When George Gershwin died, a friend of his who was a man of romantic sentiment combined with musical aspirations wrote an elegy in his honor. He took his piece to Oscar Levant who had reluctantly granted him a hearing. After eagerly playing the piece on Levant's piano he turned to his host, looking for his reaction.

"Really," sighed Levant, "I think it would have been better if you had died and Gershwin had written the elegy."

2232   PEACE CORPS AND POVERTY PROGRAMS

Paul Bell, Peace Corps Director for Central America, tells this story about Sargent Shriver when he was still handling both Peace Corps and Poverty programs. Bell sent to Shriver the nomination of a Washington attorney to direct Peace Corps work in Guatemala. Shriver approved the appointment, but added this note: "What does he know about Guatemala?"

Replied Bell in another memo: "Not much, Sarge. But what do you know about poverty?"

2233   PRETTY WEAK TEA

Joan Davis complained to a waitress that her tea looked pretty weak. "Lady," said the waitress, "you'd be weak, too, if you'd been dunked eighty-eight times in a cup of hot water."

2234   OBSERVATION ON HIS BUST

When Ralph Waldo Emerson was sitting for the sculptor, Daniel Chester French for his bust, he observed:

"The trouble is, the more it resembles me, the worse it looks."

2235   INTRODUCTION TO PHILOSOPHY COURSE—REFILLING HOLES

Morris Cohen, philosopher and educator, had reached the end of an introduction-to-philosophy course when a female student arose in the role of intellectually ravished virtue. "Professor Cohen," she declared, "you have knocked a hole in everything I've ever believed in, and you have given me nothing to take its place!"

"Young lady," Professor Cohen replied, "you will recall that among the labors of Hercules, he was required to clean out the Augean stables. He was not, let me point out, required to refill them."

2236   CAUTIOUS SPEAKER WITH SCIENTIFIC ACCURACY

Cordell Hull was well known for being an extremely cautious speaker. He was always aiming for scientific accuracy. One day while traveling on a train, a companion pointed to a fine flock of sheep grazing in a field. "Look. Those sheep have just been sheared," he noted.

Hull studied the flock and then remarked slowly: "Sheared on this side anyway."

2237   BAGGAGE INSPECTION—"JUST CLOTHES"

Returning from a trip to Europe, Mark Twain became annoyed as a customs official rummaged through his baggage. "My good friend," the author exclaimed, "you don't have to mix up all my things. There are only clothes in there—nothing but clothes."

But the suspicious fellow kept looking about until he hit upon something hard. He pulled out a quart of the finest quality bourbon. "You call this 'just clothes?' " cried the official.

"Sure thing," Twain replied calmly, "That is my nightcap!"

2238   THE MAKING OF A FOOL

When he said we were trying to make a fool of him, I could only murmur that the Creator had beat us to it.   *Ilka Chase*

2239   THANKS FOR PASSING HOUSE

James MacNeill Whistler was once seated at a dinner party opposite a well-known elderly bore. During a lull in the conversation he leaned forward toward the artist.

"Do you know, Mr. Whistler," he announced, "I passed your house this morning."

"Thank you," replied Whistler, "Thank you very much!"

2240   COMMENT TO A HECKLER

Lyndon B. Johnson tells this story: "Al Smith was addressing a crowd when a heckler yelled, "Tell 'em what's on your mind, Al. It won't take long." Smith grinned, pointed at the man and shouted, "Stand up, pardner, and I'll tell 'em what's on both our minds. It won't take any longer!"

2241   HOW CAN YOU TELL DEATH?

When Wilson Mizner was told that Calvin Coolidge was dead, he said, "How can they tell?"

SALESMEN

2242   SELLING NOVEL IN DEEP SOUTH

Emmet Dedman tells about a book salesman who was selling his line to a dealer in the deep, deep South. "Our next novel," said the salesman with an apologetic cough, "deals with the problem of, er, incest."

"That's the trouble with you Yankees," snapped the dealer, "you make a problem out of everything."

2243   BOAT BUILDER'S CLAIMS FOR GUNBOAT CONTRACT

During Civil War days, a boat builder who was trying to get a gunboat contract sought to impress Abraham Lincoln by making extravagant claims about his product. He finally said that they would run in unbelievably shallow water.

"I have no doubt of it," the President replied, "I wouldn't be surprised if they'd run anywhere as long as the ground's a little moist."

SELF-APPRAISAL

2244   TRUE GREATNESS

To feel themselves in the presence of true greatness many men find it necessary only to be alone.   *Tom Masson*

2245   BEGINNING OF LONG ROMANCE

To love one's self is the beginning of a life-long romance.   *Oscar Wilde*

2246   SELF-LOVE

He was like a cock who thought the sun had risen to hear him crow.
George Eliot

2247   DISCHARGE OF OBLIGATION

When some men discharge an obligation, you can hear the report for miles around.   *Mark Twain*

2248   IDEA OF AN AGREEABLE PERSON

My idea of an agreeable person is one who agrees with me.
Dr. Samuel Johnson

2249   REASON FOR SINGING WHEN SAD

Mark Twain said, "When I'm sad I sing, and then others can be sad with me."

2250   NO PROOF IN NOISE

Noise proves nothing; often a hen who has merely laid an egg cackles as if she had laid an asteroid.   *Mark Twain*

STUDENTS

2251   STOREHOUSE OF KNOWLEDGE

Harvard University is conceded to be one of the nation's greatest storehouses of knowledge, and its one-time president, the late Charles W. Eliot, had a ready explanation. "We're adding more knowledge every semester," he declared. "The freshmen bring us so much of it—and the seniors take away so little!"

2252   TYPES OF COLLEGE GRADUATES

Some men are graduated from college *cum laude*, some are graduated *summa cum laude*, and some are graduated *mirabile dictu*.

2253   STUDENT RESPONSIBLE FOR TOP HALF OF CLASS

When A. Whitney Griswold was president of Yale, he told about a student who was asked by the dean whether he was in the top half of his class.

"Oh, no sir," responded the student. "I'm one of those who make the top half possible."

2254   COLLEGE STUDENTS' VOICE—PAST AND PRESENT

Bob Hope remembers when college students had something to say. "They wanted to stand up and be counted," he recalls. "but now they want to sit down and be carried."

SUCCESS

2255   WHEN TO QUIT TRYING

If at first you don't succeed, try, try again. Then quit. There's no use being a damn fool about it.   *W. C. Fields*

2256   END OF BALL GAME PLAYED IN COW PASTURE

William Faulkner recalls a ball game once played in Mississippi. It was being successfully played in a cow pasture but ended abruptly when a runner slid into what he thought was third base.

2257   LIVING ON SMALL INCOME

It's not too hard to live on a small income if you don't spend too much time trying to keep it a secret.   *Arthur Godfrey*

2258   TIME TO QUIT PRO-FOOTBALL

Charles Conerly, the former Giants' quarterback who retired from pro-football when he was 40, told Toots Shor how he suddenly decided it was time to quit. It was after curfew at training camp and he was in bed, when he said to himself: "There's something silly about a 40-year-old man *having* to be in bed before 11 P.M."

2259   VALUE OF FAITH

You can do very little with faith, but you can do nothing without it.

Samuel Butler

2260   WITH OR WITHOUT CHARM

If you have charm, you don't need to have anything else; and if you don't have it, it doesn't matter what else you have.   *James Mathew Barrie*

2261   FORMULA FOR SUCCESS

Einstein, asked for the secret of his success, said, "If A is success in life, I should say that the formula for success is A equals X plus Y plus Z, with X standing for work and Y for play. But what is Z? That is keeping your mouth shut."

2262   AMOUNT OF SUFFERING

I have suffered from being misunderstood, but I would have suffered a hell of a lot more if I had been understood.   *Clarence Darrow*

2263   A DIPLOMAT'S COMPLAINT

A diplomat once complained to Talleyrand that he could not understand why he was considered ill-natured, adding, "In all my life I have done but one ill-natured action."

Replied Talleyrand, "And when will it end?"

2264   TV—MEDIUM RARE

Television is called a medium because anything good on it is rare.   *Fred Allen*

2265   PREFERENCE FOR DYING OR THINKING

Most people would sooner die than think; in fact, they do so.   *Bertrand Russell*

2266   QUIT SMOKING—EASIEST THING IN THE WORLD

To cease smoking is the easiest thing in the world; I ought to know because I've done it a thousand times.   *Mark Twain*

WEALTH

2267 LIVING UP TO THE JONES'S

When a suburban husband asked his wife why they never had any money, she said: "It's the neighbors, dear. They are always doing something we can't afford."

Walter Winchell

2268 THINGS TO DO IN A COMFORTABLE POSITION

I wish I were either rich enough or poor enough to do a lot of things that are impossible in my present comfortable circumstances. *Don Herold*

2269 WATCHING THE BASKET

Put all your eggs in one basket, and—watch that basket! *Mark Twain*

2270 DIVIDING AN INHERITANCE

Never say you know a man until you have divided an inheritance with him.

Johann Kaspar Lavater

WEATHER

2271 NEW ENGLAND WEATHER

If you don't like the weather in New England, just wait a few minutes.

Mark Twain

WOMEN

2272 DIET-CONSCIOUS LADY

A diet-conscious lady once weighed 186 pounds, but she went on a strict diet. Now she weighs only 85 pounds, including the casket. *Joey Adams*

2273   DOCTOR'S PREFERENCE FOR SILENT WOMEN

Dr. Johnson was one day in conversation with a very talkative lady, of whom he appeared to take very little notice. "Why doctor, I believe you prefer the company of men to that of the ladies."

"Madam," replied he. "I am very fond of the company of ladies; I like their beauty, I like their delicacy. I like their vivacity, and I like their silence."

2274   BOB HOPE'S THOUGHTS ON DOROTHY LAMOUR IN A SARONG

Somebody asked Bob Hope what went through his mind when he got his original view of Dorothy Lamour in a sarong. "I never gave it a second thought," he averred. "I was too busy with the first one."

2275   EYES FOCUSED ON PAPAL NUNCIO

Pope John XXIII lived in Paris for some years as a papal nuncio. There he acquired a considerable reputation as a wit. One of his more memorable quotes: "I have noticed," he told a dinner table companion, "that if a woman arrives wearing a gown that is cut rather daringly low, everybody gazes not at the woman, but at me."

2276   DESCRIPTION OF WOMEN'S PREACHING

A woman's preaching is like a dog's walking on his hind legs; it is not done well, but you are surprised to find it done at all.   *Dr. Samuel Johnson*

2277   MEANING OF WOMAN DRIVER STICKING OUT HER HAND

When a woman driver sticks out her hand to make a turn, it means only one thing: the window is open.   *Arthur Godfrey*

2278   GIFTS FROM PERFECT STRANGERS

Zsa Zsa Gabor quips, "I don't take gifts from perfect strangers—but then, nobody's perfect."

2279   POWER OF WOMEN

Nature has given women so much power that the law has very wisely given them little.   *Samuel Johnson*

2280   BEGINNING OF LIKING GIRLS

A Hollywood reporter asked Gene Kelly, "When did you first begin to like girls?" Replied Kelly, "The minute I discovered they weren't boys."

2281   APPRAISAL OF WOMEN

Women may not be much, but they are the best other sex we have.

Don Herold

2282   AWARENESS OF WOMEN

Women are perfectly well aware that the more they seem to obey the more they rule.   *Michelet*

2283   RETREATING FEMALES

The females of all species are most dangerous when they appear to retreat.

2284   THE BARKING BOSOM—GOING THROUGH CUSTOMS

The celebrated actress, Mrs. Patrick Campbell, was traveling with her tiny white Pekingese, Moonbeam. In describing her encounter with certain port officers, she recalled: "I knew the law, of course, but I knew how poor little dogs suffer away from their masters. Moonbeam trusted me so; I couldn't betray him. I made up my mind to take him through with me.

"So I tucked him into my bosom and covered him with my cape. I smiled my prettiest. I sailed up to the barrier. Everything was going splendidly—until my bosom barked."

2285   POWER OF SPEECH

She had lost the art of conversation, but not, unfortunately, the power of speech.

George Bernard Shaw

2286   WIFE'S UNDERSTANDING OF HER HUSBAND'S THEORIES

Mrs. Albert Einstein was asked, one day, if she understood her husband's theories. She replied: "I understand the words, but I don't always understand the sentences."

2287   MISTAKING A BULGE FOR A CURVE

An optimist is a girl who mistakes a bulge for a curve.   *Ring Lardner*

2288   OPINION ON MINISKIRTS

Asked his opinion of miniskirts at a press conference, New York's Mayor, John V. Lindsay, replied, "It's a functional thing. It enables young ladies to run faster, and because of it, they may have to."

2289   SHAKESPEARE'S MASTERPIECES—COMPOSED BY QUEEN ELIZABETH

Harvey Breit tells about a long-haired scholar from Wisconsin who insisted that Shakespeare's plays had been written by Queen Elizabeth. The eminent minister, Dr. Hugh Black, challenged him. "Surely," he scoffed, "you don't believe a woman could have composed such masterpieces." "You miss my point entirely," said the scholar. "It is my contention that Queen Elizabeth was a man."

WORDS

2290   ECONOMY OF WORDS

I know only two tunes; one of them is "Yankee Doodle" and the other isn't.
                                                                Ulysses S. Grant

2291   SILENT COOLIDGE AND CONVERSATIONALIST AT DINNER PARTY

When Coolidge was Vice-President, he was invited to attend many dinners. Always he was the despair of his hostess because of his utter disregard of the art of conversation. One lady felt that she had solved this problem by placing him next to Alice Roosevelt Longworth who was a most brilliant conversationalist.

Mrs. Longworth began to chat in her usual charming fashion, but failed to elicit any response from the silent Mr. Coolidge. Finally, exasperated out of her generally calm demeanor, she acidly asked, "You go to so many dinners. They must bore you a great deal."

Calmly Coolidge replied without lifting his eyes from the contemplation of the plate before him, "Well, a man has to eat somewhere."

2292   UNSAID WORDS

I have never been hurt by anything I didn't say.   *Calvin Coolidge*

2293   REPETITION OF ANYTHING

If you don't say anything, you won't be called on to repeat it.   *Calvin Coolidge*

2294   SMALL BOY'S ACCOUNT OF ELIJAH

Mark Twain enjoyed telling the story of the small boy's account of Elijah in his less ingratiating mood.

The boy would tell, "There was a prophet named Elijah. One day he was going up a mountainside. Some boys threw stones at him. So he said, 'If you keep on throwing stones at me I'll set the bears on you and they'll eat you up.' And they did, and he did, and the bears did."

WORK

2295   FASCINATION OF WORK

I like work; it fascinates me. I can sit and look at it for hours.
                                                    Jerome K. Jerome

2296   WORKING PEOPLE AT THE VATICAN

When asked by a reporter how many people work in the Vatican, Pope John XXIII answered good-naturedly, "About half!"

2297   QUICKNESS OF MOVEMENT

Why did the Lord give us so much quickness of movement unless it was to avoid responsibility.   *Ogden Nash*

2298   SUBJECT OF CLOTHES

Clarence Darrow was a hard working and energetic man. His clothes were often disheveled. Once he was ragged about this by a group of reporters. He silenced them by saying, "I go to a better tailor than any of you and pay more money for my clothes. The only difference between us is that you probably don't sleep in yours."

2299   DEFINITION OF A GENIUS

Genius is one percent inspiration and ninety-nine percent perspiration!
T. A. Edison

2300   WILLING PEOPLE IN THE WORLD

The world is full of willing people; some willing to work, the rest willing to let them.   *Robert Frost*

2301   TAUGHT TO WORK—NOT TO LOVE IT

My father taught me to work; he did not teach me to love it.
Abraham Lincoln

2302   BEING A BOSS—WITH INCREASING WORK HOURS

By working faithfully, eight hours a day, you may eventually get to be a boss and work twelve hours a day.   *Robert Frost*

2303   HOW TO HAVE A BEAUTIFUL GARDEN—WORK

Gardens are not made by singing "Oh, how beautiful," and sitting in the shade.
Rudyard Kipling

2304   TWO REASONS FOR DOING THINGS

A man always has two reasons for doing anything—a good reason and the real reason.   *J. Pierpont Morgan*

2305   DEFINITION OF A VICE-PRESIDENT

A vice-president is a person who finds a molehill on his desk in the morning and must make a mountain out of it by five.   *Fred Allen*

2306   BUSY BEE

A bee is never as busy as it seems; it's just that it can't buzz any slower.
Frank McKinney Hubbard

2307   THINGS BEING DONE IN A FAST MOVING WORLD

The world is moving so fast these days that the man who says it can't be done is generally interrupted by someone doing it.   *Elbert Hubbard*

2308   THE WORKING OF A BRAIN

The brain is a wonderful organ; it starts working the moment you get up in the morning and does not stop until you get into the office.   *Robert Frost*

2309   NO ENTHUSIASM FOR MOUNTAIN CLIMBING

G. K. Chesterton could work up no enthusiasm for mountain climbing. He is reported to have said: "I will lift up mine eyes unto the hills, but I know of no particular reason why I must lift my carcass up there also."

2310   USE OF STEAM

Steam is no stronger now than it was a hundred years ago, but it is put to better use.   *Emerson*

WRITERS

2311   HOLLYWOOD WRITER'S ATTIRE

I'm a Hollywood writer, so I put on a sports jacket and take off my brain.
                                                                   Ben Hecht

2312   GHOST WRITING STANDARDS

At one time Samuel Goldwyn hired a ghost writer to do a series of articles purported to be by Goldwyn. The writer became ill and one of the pieces was done by a substitute ghost. Upon reading this piece Goldwyn expressed considerable dismay and said, "This is not up to my usual standard."

2313   THE MEDIOCRE WRITER

Only a mediocre writer is always at his best.   *William Somerset Maugham*

ADVERTISING

3001   ADVISABILITY OF HIRING PRESS AGENTS

A smart young man tried to sell a successful manufacturer on the desirability of hiring him as press agent. Said the manufacturer: "Our company is the biggest in its field, and therefore what it does, and what I do, is news." But the young man was not to be put off.

"Ever hear of Napoleon?" he asked.

"Of course," said the business man.

"How about Wellington?" continued the job hunter.

"Let's see," was the answer, "didn't he have something to do with the Battle of Waterloo?"

"There you are," the young man came back. "Wellington was the man who didn't need a press agent. He beat the pants off Napoleon at the Battle of Waterloo, but it's Napoleon you always hear of. He had a press agent."

3002   BACKING UP ADVERTISEMENT'S CLAIMS WITH THE GOODS

In making a point about the advisability of advertising, the following story also illustrates the importance of being able to back up your advertisement's claims.

An elephant met a lion in the jungle and asked, "Why do you make such a fool of yourself by roaring so much?"

"Oh, there's a good reason for it," replied the lion jovially. "They call me the King of the Beasts because I *advertise*."

A rabbit, hiding in the brush, overheard this conversation and was deeply impressed. He thought he would try the lion's strategy and when he encountered a fox tried to roar like the lion but—it came out a tiny squeak. The unimpressed fox had himself a meal in the woods, reminding himself in the process that it does not pay to advertise unless you have the goods!

3003   VILLAGE GROCER—LOCAL PAPER SALESMAN—RINGING THE BELL

A representative from a local paper was seeking advertisements and he called at the village grocer's. Upon presenting his card, he was surprised when the gray-haired proprietor said: "Nothing doing. Been established 80 years and never advertised."

Asked the salesman: "Excuse me, sir, but what is that building on the hill?"

Replied the grocer: "The village church."

Asked the salesman: "Has it been there long?"

"Oh—about 200 years."

"Well," was the reply, "they still ring the bell!"

3004   SALES MANAGER AND AD MANAGER DISCUSSING ORDER ON BOOKS

Thundered a sales manager to the advertising manager, "I defy you to show me one order that advertising ever put on our books."

Replied the ad manager, "I will just as soon as you can show me a single load of hay that the sun ever put in a barn."

3005   FLEA STUDY

This joke is currently the favorite in the Madison Avenue advertising agencies: An account executive was told to provide an exhaustive study about fleas. He laboriously trained a medium-sized flea to jump over his finger every time he said "Hup." Then he pulled off two of the flea's six legs. "Hup," he grunted. The flea jumped over his finger. Off came two more legs. "Hup," repeated the executive. Again the flea jumped. Then he pulled off the flea's last two legs. Alas, the flea no longer moved. The executive nodded sagely and wrote in his report: "When a flea loses all six of its legs, it becomes deaf."

3006   DIFFERENCE BETWEEN ENDORSING AND SMOKING CIGARETTES

The famous tenor, Giovanni Martinelli, was once asked if he smoked. "Tobacco! I would not think of it!" said the singer. "But," said one of the reporters, "didn't you once endorse a cigarette and say that it did not irritate your throat." "Of course I endorsed it, and it is true that the cigarettes did not hurt my throat. I never smoked them."

ADVICE

3007   ANYBODY'S AND EVERYBODY'S ADVICE

Advice can certainly be of use, but this anecdote brings home a good point on the subject:

Two broken-down old men sat on a park bench. One said, "I'm here because I *never* took advice from anybody."

"Shake," said the other man, "I'm here because I took everybody's advice."

3008   LEADING A GOOD CHRISTIAN LIFE

"Can I lead a good Christian life in New York City on $15 a week?" a young man once asked a well-known New York minister.

"My boy," was the reply, "that's all you can do."

3009   HUSBAND AND WIFE HELPING EACH OTHER

A husband drew his chair beside his wife's sewing machine.

"Don't you think you're running too fast?" he said. "Look out! You'll sew the wrong seam! Mind that corner, now! Slow down, watch your fingers! Steady!"

"What's the matter with you, John?" said his wife, alarmed, "I've been running this machine for years!"

"Well, dear" replied the husband, "I thought you might like me to help you, since you help me drive the car."

3010   PLEASE KEEP THE SHOWER CURTAINS ON THE INSIDE

At an annual hotel owners' convention a roving commentator, mike in hand, approached a world-famous hotel man. Holding up the mike, he said, "Sir, your name has become synonymous with the hotel business. You have expanded your chain to all corners of the globe, offering the peoples of the world a comfortable 'home away from home.' Do you have a word, sir? All America is listening and watching!"

"Yes, thank you," said the hotel magnate. "I do have a word for all America. Please keep the shower curtains on the inside!"

3011   HELPFUL HINTS FROM RINGMASTER

A beautiful and adventurous girl ran away from home and joined the circus. "I don't want to make the usual beginner's mistakes," she told the ringmaster. "Can you give me a few helpful hints?"

"Well, for one thing," mused the ringmaster, "don't ever undress around the bearded lady."

BIGOTRY

3012   BIGOTED BLUE-BLOOD—ANCESTORS OF

A cloak and suit manufacturer, obviously born abroad, was taunted on his Americanism by a bigoted blue-blood.

"What kind of American are you, after all?" sneered the blue-blood. "Why, my ancestors came over on the Mayflower."

The cloak and suit man, unperturbed, replied, "Maybe it's lucky they did. By the time I arrived, the immigration laws were a lot stricter."

3013   RUNNING FOR CLUB'S PRESIDENCY—MEMBERSHIP COMMITTEE'S DECEPTION

The reactionary members of an exclusive club had resorted to every underhanded method to reject the application bid of John Riley because they looked down on the ex-bricklayer, although he had become a millionaire. However, he had sufficient friends in the organization to insure his admission. He soon became extremely popular and was prevailed upon to run for the club's presidency against a representative of the reactionary group. Unfortunately, the vote was tied and both candidates agreed to pull a slip from a box which was to contain one card marked "winner" and one marked "loser." The membership committee was controlled by his enemies who decided to mark both cards with the word "loser" and force him to draw first. At the last minute, Riley was informed of the deception by a friend.

"Aren't you going to make a complaint and have the election declared invalid?" he was asked.

"Sure, and I'll do nothing about it," he answered cheerfully. At the drawing, he pulled out a card, read it, tore it into tiny pieces and walked away chuckling.

"Hold on there," said the angry election chairman. "What was written on your card?"

"Don't bother about that," urged Riley, "just read what's on the card that's left."

3014   GROUPS OF PEOPLE

People are divided into two groups—the ignorant, illogical, prejudiced, emotional group, and the intelligent, sound-thinking, reasonable people like us.

BUSINESS

3015 THE DAY OF REST—FOR THE CREATOR AND THE FARMER

The executive was on his way to the country club one Sunday morning for a game of golf when in a field he noticed an elderly farmer whom he knew.

"Say, John," he asked, "don't you know that the Creator made the world in only six days and that he rested on the seventh?"

"I know all about that," said the farmer, as he glanced up. "But He got done and I didn't."

3016 UNSOLICITED MANUSCRIPT—OPENING LINE

A publisher in Indianapolis received an unsolicited manuscript entitled, "How to Make Your Own Mink Coat." The opening line was, "First, catch sixty-two minks."

3017 A RED BANDANA AND FIFTY YEARS OF SERVICE TO THE COMMUNITY

"This here town has been mighty good to me," boomed the guest of honor at a reception signalizing his fifty years of service to the community. "When I first arrived here, I was an inexperienced tenderfoot with only one suit on my back and all my worldly possessions wrapped in a red bandana over my shoulder. Today, I own the bank, the newspaper, the two hotels, nine oil wells, and the TV station!"

Later, an impressed visitor asked, "Would you tell us just what was in that bandana when you arrived here fifty years ago?"

"Let's see now," mused the guest of honor. "If I recall rightly, I was carrying about $400,000 in cash and $750,000 in negotiable securities."

3018 ANNOUNCING A BANK ROBBERY

In a large city bank one afternoon, a little old lady was startled as policemen suddenly appeared and seized a man in front of one of the windows. Going to the manager, she inquired what was happening. The manager explained that they had a tip-off about a planned robbery and had been waiting for the thief when he came into the bank.

"Well, really," said the little old lady, "at least you could have told us in advance so that we could watch."

3019   IMPROVING BUSINESS—ONE WAY OR ANOTHER

Business was way below par in a certain men's furnishings shop, and the proprietor, in desperation, tried to haul in a passer-by.

"I already have thirty-two suits in my wardrobe."

"O.K.," proposed the proprietor, "I have another proposition. Bring the suits in and I'll make you my partner."

3020   TIGER AND SHEEP NOVELTY ACT

Biggest gross for an animal act at a Midwestern carnival was rung up by a novelty: a tiger and a sheep performing tricks in the same cage.

"Amazing," commented a visitor. "Do those oddly assorted creatures always get along so amiably together?"

"They do have a bit of a dust-up every now and then," admitted the trainer, "but we don't let that bother us. We just buy a new sheep."

3021   NOISE OF ONE FORLORN FROG SKIN

A New England manufacturer was in the market for bull frog skins, and a Texan promptly wrote that he could supply any quantity up to 100,000. "Send them all," invited the manufacturer.

A few days later, one forlorn frog skin arrived with this attached to the box: "Turned out this is all the frog skins there was. The noise sure fooled me!"

3022   SALES MANAGER'S WARNING TO SALEMAN

The sales manager of a fast-growing outfit sticks pins in a big relief map behind his desk to show where everyone of his salesmen is at a given moment. Ragsdale, of the New England sector, was not, in the opinion of the manager, living up to his early promise, and was summoned to the home office for a pep talk and reindoctrination. "I'm not saying you're in imminent danger yet of being fired," was the stern finale of the sales manager's warning, "but, if you'll look carefully at my map, Ragsdale, you'll note I've loosened your pin!"

3023   COMPANY'S PART IN WAR EFFORT

The executive was asked what part his company had played in the war effort. "See that big plane over there? Well, we make the clips that hold the blueprints together."

3024   THE WORK BREAK TO AVOID BANKRUPTCY

Someone in the upper echelon of a California aircraft plant had sufficient sense of humor to post this notice on the bulletin board:

"To all Employees: Due to increased competition and a keen desire to avoid bankruptcy, we find it necessary to institute a new policy. Effective immediately, we are asking that somewhere between starting and quitting time and without infringing too much on the time devoted to lunch period, coffee breaks, rest period, story telling, ticket selling, golfing, auto racing, vacation planning, and rehashing of yesterday's TV programs, that each employee try to find some time that can be set aside and be known as *The Work Break*. To some, this may seem a radical innovation, but we honestly believe the idea has possibilities. It may even keep us all in business a few years longer!"

The Management

3025   MORE VICE-PRESIDENTS THAN DEPOSITORS

A man working as a teller in a bank bumped into an old friend of his one day. Seeing that the bank teller seemed very preoccupied, the friend said, "What is the matter with you?"

"Well, there is a lot of trouble down at the bank. We are going through a complete reorganization."

"Why?"

"It seems that we had more vice-presidents than depositors," replied the bank teller as he walked away.

CHILDREN

3026   DRAWING A PICTURE OF GOD

The little five-year-old was sitting at a table concentrating on a drawing. Now and then she held it up, scrutinizing it carefully, put it back, then went to work on it again.

"What are you drawing, dear?" asked her mother.

"I am drawing God," she announced.

The mother was shocked. "Why, darling, you can't draw God. No one really knows what He looks like!"

"Well," said the little girl complacently, "they will as soon as I finish."

3027   CARELESS DAD LEAVING MONEY ON RESTAURANT TABLE

A Stanford University professor took his young son with him on a trip across the country. One day after their return, a package was delivered with postage due.

Neither the professor nor his wife had the necessary $3, but their son produced it. Surprised, his mother asked how he came to have that much money. "Well," he said, "Dad was awfully careless with money on our trip and nearly always left some on the table when we ate. So I just picked it up."

3028   NEW MATH—TWO PLUS THREE IS PURPLE

Anne entered first grade last year, and soon came home telling everybody about the New Math. She brought home colored rods of graduated sizes and practiced her math with great enthusiasm. Red was twice as long as blue, orange three times as long, green four times, etc. Her father asked Anne what two plus three was, and she replied, "Two plus three is purple."

3029   IMPORTANCE OF BEING A VIRGIN OR AN ANGEL

The two young daughters of a friend of mine had been given parts in a Christmas play at school. At dinner that night they got into an argument as to who had the more important role. Judy, aged eleven, was very superior.

"Why, of course mine's the biggest part," she told five-year-old Lucy. Anybody'll tell you it's much harder to be a virgin than an angel."

3030   TEACHER'S QUESTION TO CLASS ABOUT BIRDS

The first graders were on a field trip to observe the birds beginning their migration. Explaining that the birds were noisy and excited because they were going on a long journey, the teacher asked the class, "What do you suppose they are saying?"

"I imagine," said one little girl shyly, "that the mother birds are telling their children they'd better go to the bathroom before they start."

3031   ADMINISTERING ARTIFICIAL RESPIRATION—BROTHER KEEPS GETTING UP AND WALKING AWAY

Two Cub Scouts whose younger brother had fallen into a shallow pond rushed home to Mother with tears in their eyes. "We're trying to give him artificial respiration," one of them sobbed. "But he keeps getting up and walking away."

3032   SPECIAL HAT FOR COLLEGE REUNION—ICE BAG ATOP FATHER'S HEAD

Small fry to friend, explaining ice bag atop father's head: "Mom says it's a special hat his class wears to show that they've been to their college reunion."

3033   CANDIDATES WANTED DEAD OR ALIVE

In the fall of an election year, pictures of candidates appear almost everywhere. Several were on display recently on the window of a local filling station. As we were leaving the station, seven-year-old Timmie asked, "Dad, are those guys wanted dead or alive?"

3034   WRESTLING IN A PLAYPEN

My little girl, seemingly entranced with a wrestling match on TV, finally looked up and said: "Look at those two men fighting in their playpen."

3035   VISIT TO A DEAD CIRCUS

As a special treat, a teacher took her class to visit the museum of natural history. The children returned home very excitedly, and rushing into his house, one of the little boys greeted his mother exuberantly, saying, "What do you think we did today, Mother! The teacher took us to a dead circus."

3036   GOING TO GOD'S HOUSE—FELLOW WAS NEVER THERE

Rebuking her small son for not going to church willingly, his mother said, "You go to the movies for entertainment and you go down to Freddie's house, and over to Timmie's house, and you have a nice time. Now don't you think it is only right that once a week you should go to God's House, just for one hour?"

The boy thought it over and said, "But Mom, what would you think if you were invited to somebody's house and every time you went, the fellow was never there!"

3037   THERE GOES THE LORD'S NICKEL

A young hopeful, setting out for Sunday School one morning, was given two nickels, one for the collection plate and one for himself. As he was rambling down the street he played with the coins. One of them slipped out of his hand, rolled away from him and disappeared irretrievably into the sewer. The youngster gazed ruefully down through the grate for a moment, and then said, "Well, there goes the Lord's nickel."

3038   LITTLE BROTHER AND HIS SLED—WHERE'S HIS SLED?

The day of a big snowstorm, the country school teacher felt called upon to warn her charges against playing too long in the snow. She said, "Now, children, you must be careful about colds and over-exposure. I had a darling little brother only seven years old. One day he went out in the snow with his new sled and caught cold. Pneumonia set in and three days later he died."

The room was silent and then a youngster in the back row raised his hand and asked, "Where's his sled?"

3039   SINGING AT SUNDAY SCHOOL

A little boy had been to Sunday school for the first time, and when asked what they did, he said: "Everybody sang."

"What did they sing? asked his mother.

"I don't know what the rest of them sang," he informed her, "but *I* sang 'Casey Jones.' "

3040   A BARKING DOG NEVER BITES—DOG'S KNOWLEDGE OF PROVERB

A little boy was very worried by a vicious looking dog.

"Don't be afraid of him," the owner reassured him. "You know the old proverb, 'A barking dog never bites.' "

"Yes," replied the boy, "I do know the proverb, and you know the proverb, but does the dog know the proverb?"

3041   ANNOUNCING NEW BABY AT HOME

Little Johnny announced to his grocer that there was a new baby at his home. "Is he going to stay?" the grocer asked.

"I guess so," replied Johnny, "he's got all his things off."

3042   HIRING LITTLE BROTHER AS SERVANT—PAY, DON'T RAISE IT ANY LOWER

Nine-year-old Henry struck upon the idea of hiring his little brother as his servant. "I'll give you ten cents a week," he said.

"O.K.," little Tom agreed.

Henry then felt he'd offered too much money. "I can only pay you five cents a week, after all!" he said.

"O.K.," said Tom, just as cheerfully.

Henry, thinking then he could get the child for even less, said, "All I can pay is a penny a week."

"Well, O.K.," said Tom, "but don't raise it any lower!"

3043   THE WAITRESS THINKS THE LITTLE BOY IS REAL

A family was seated in a restaurant. The waitress took the order of the adults and then turned to their young son.

"What will you have, sonny?" she asked .

The boy said timidly, "I want a hot dog."

Before the waitress could write down the order, the mother interrupted.

"No hot dog," she said. "Give him potatoes, beef and some carrots." But the waitress ignored her completely.

"Do you want some ketchup or mustard on your hot dog?" she asked of the boy.

"Ketchup," he replied with a happy smile on his face.

"Coming up," the waitress said, starting for the kitchen.

There was a stunned silence upon her departure. Finally, the boy turned to his parents. "Know what?" he said, "She thinks I'm *real*!"

3044   SOMETHING EXTRA—MOUTH SOAPER

One small boy was overheard saying the following to a friend: "That tongue twister you taught me was also a mouth soaper."

3045   FOUR-YEAR-OLD GIVES ADVICE TO FATHER

A San Francisco father blew up while trying to mediate the usual family hassle around the dinner table. "Everybody wants his own way around here!" he hollered. "Me, I'm just the poor schnook of a father. When do I get *my* way for once?" Four-year-old Mark tugged at his sleeve and suggested, "Cry a little."

3046   BOYS PASSING THE TIME OF DAY—FINDING OUT ABOUT DIFFERENCE IN AGE

Two small boys were swinging on a gate together, passing the time of day. One asked the other, "How old are you?"

"Five," the other replied. "How old are you?"

"I don't know," said the first.

"You don't know how old you are?"

"No."

"Do women bother you?"

"No."

"Then you're four."

3047   NEW SHOES—ON WRONG FEET

Six-year-old Mary was crying bitterly. Her mother asked what was the matter. "My new shoes hurt!"

Replied her mother: "No wonder, dear. You have them on the wrong feet."

The little girl stopped crying and thought for a moment, then said: "But Mommy —I haven't any other feet."

3048   BAREFOOT DAUGHTER AND MODEL

The daughter of a famous American artist had a passion for flitting about barefoot, but her mother frowned on the practice. "You're getting to be a grown-up young lady, now," she pointed out, "and I insist that you wear shoes."

One morning the daughter ignored the "Keep Out" sign on the door of her father's studio, and came upon him painting a model in the nude. She raced right to her mother, and announced triumphantly, "You see, Mamma? *She's* allowed to go barefoot!"

3049   FIRST DAY AT KINDERGARTEN—FINDING OUT DIFFERENCE BETWEEN BOY AND GIRL

Five-year-old Peter came home from his first day at Kindergarten to face a quiz from his father. "Do you like the other boys in the class?"

"You bet."

"And the girls?"

Peter registered disgust. "Come now," pleaded Papa, "you like Judy just a little, don't you?"

Peter registered astonishment. "Don't tell me," he pleaded, "that Judy is a GIRL!"

3050   KINDERGARTEN TEACHER'S INSPIRATIONAL TALK—SMALL BOY'S PROTEST

The day-before-Christmas festivities were particularly gay at P.S. 10, and the kindergarten teacher decided to conclude the program with a short inspirational talk. "The spirit of brotherly love and good fellowship rule in America, not only at Yuletide but all through the year," she declared, "and that is because all of us are FREE." At this point, a small boy in the back of the room protested vigorously: "I'm NOT free; I'm FOUR."

3051   EARNING CAPACITIES OF RESPECTIVE FATHERS— BOYS BOASTING ABOUT

The boys fell to boasting about the earning capacities of their respective fathers. Said the doctor's son, 'My pa operated on a movie producer last month and sent him a bill for a cool five thousand." The lawyer's son spoke up, "Shucks, what's that? My old man was the mouthpiece for a big racketeer a week ago and got a fee of ten grand for one day's work—all paid in crisp new thousand-dollar bills." The minister's son said quietly, "On Sunday, my father preached a sermon in church and it took eight men to bring in the money."

3052   EDUCATIONAL TOY—COMPLICATED

The young mother examined the toy rather dubiously and asked the salesman, "Isn't this rather complicated for a small child?"

Replied the clerk, "It's an educational toy, madam. It's designed to adjust a child to live in the world of today. Any way he puts it together, it's wrong."

3053   ST. PETER AND EMPTY CIGAR BOX—PET PARAKEET GOING TO HEAVEN

Little Agnes was inconsolable; her pet parakeet had died suddenly. To comfort her, her father suggested that they bury the bird in an empty cigar box in the backyard. They made a little marker for the grave and covered it with flowers. This diversion seemed to cheer her for a while.

Suddenly, the little girl asked her father, "Daddy, do you think my little parakeet will go to heaven?"

"He was a good little bird. I'm pretty sure he will."

"But Daddy," murmured the child in a querulous tone, "I'm so afraid that when St. Peter opens the box and finds it isn't cigars after all, he'll be very very mad!"

3054   DUST TO DUST

On the way home from church on Ash Wednesday, little Johnny queried his mother: "Is it true, Mommy, that we are made of dust?"

"Yes, darling."

"And do we go back to dust again when we die?"

"Yes, dear."

"Well, Mommy, when I said my prayers last night and looked under the bed, I found someone who is either coming or going!"

3055   SANTA CLAUS—BELIEVING IN

A seven-year-old asked his friend if he believes in Santa Claus.

"Yes. Don't you?"

"Nope."

"Why not?"

"I'm too young. My daddy told my mommy the only people who believe in Santa are elevator operators, doormen, janitors, and letter carriers. And I'm too young to work yet!"

3056   A PENNY FOR YOUR THOUGHTS—YOUNG MOTHER TO HUSBAND

A young mother looked in the nursery one evening and saw her husband standing silently by the crib, looking down thoughtfully. In his face she could read his wonder and admiration, and she went to him softly and took his hand in hers and said, "A penny for your thoughts."

He looked at her and said, "I can't understand it. How on earth can the manufacturer make a crib like this for $15.95?"

3057   VISIT TO ZOO—STORY ABOUT

Admonished a mother to her small child, "Now, don't tell stories, Jimmy. You know your father has never taken you to the zoo."

"But, Mommy, yes he did! And one of the animals paid twenty-seven dollars."

3058   QUADRUPLETS AND "FIFTH"

After his wife had quadruplets, he went out and bought a fifth.

3059   CHEERFUL GIVER

Children always have a way to justify their actions. One father, wishing very much to develop his son's character, gave him a penny and a quarter as he was departing for church saying, "Now, son, you put whichever one you want in the collection plate."

When the young boy returned home, the father asked which coin he had given. The boy replied, "Well, just before they sent the plate around the preacher said, 'The Lord loveth a cheerful giver,' and I know I could be a lot more cheerful if I gave the penny, so I gave it."

3060   BABY SITTER FOR JESUS

Family life these days is a far cry from what it used to be. A little seven-year-old girl was shown a reproduction of Leonardo da Vinci's famous "Virgin and the Christ Child." Explained the mother, "That is Jesus when he was a baby." "Who's that holding Him?" asked the youngster. "A sitter?"

3061   DEAD TEEN-AGER—MOMMY LOOKING LIKE

A woman was about to leave her house wearing a mini skirt, fishnet stockings, poor boy sweater, plastic earrings and white lipstick. At the door her little daughter looked her up and down, then exclaimed, "Mommy, you look like a dead teen-ager!"

3062   MUSICAL FORMS—CONDUCTOR DEFINING

A small boy was taken to a concert of classical music for children. The conductor took the trouble to explain various musical forms to his young audience.

Among these forms was swing, which he defined as an unconventional and irregular movement from bar to bar. Whereat the small boy was heard to exclaim, "My pop calls that a bender."

3063   TWIN BROTHERS AND GOD

A pastor greeted the little girl warmly: "Good morning, May, I hear God has seen fit to send you two little twin brothers."

She replied, "Yes, sir. He knows where the money's coming from too. I heard Daddy say so."

3064   DAD AND HIS TUXEDO

The young boy watched with growing apprehension as his father changed from a business suit into a tuxedo. Finally, the youngster could hold it no longer and he blurted out.

"Dad, please don't wear that suit. It always gives you a headache the next day."

3065   BOY AT A SEANCE—TALKING TO HIS GRANDFATHER

A staunch believer in telepathic spiritualism took her eight-year-old son to a seance. The medium had great talent, and in a moment the assemblage entered a trancelike state. That is, all but the boy. "I want to talk to my grandfather," he announced loudly.

"Hush," warned the medium.

"I will not. I want to talk to my grandfather," the boy persisted.

"Oh, very well." The medium gestured grandiosely and an apparition appeared against a black backdrop. "Here's your grandfather."

"Hi ya, Grandpa," the boy called. "Whadda you doing up there? You ain't dead."

3066   TURKEY AND STUFFING

A young boy upon being offered some roast turkey, specified that he wanted the drumstick. After being served this, his mother asked him, "Wouldn't you like some of this nice stuffing?" The boy replied immediately, "No, thank you!" And after a thoughtful moment added, "And I don't see why the turkeys eat it either."

3067   WHERE ARE THE PARENTS?

A graduate student working on juvenile delinquency reported in a Wisconsin University sociology seminar that he was having difficulty in collecting data. His project was to telephone a dozen homes around 9 P.M. and ask the parents if they knew where their children were at this hour.

"My first five calls," he lamented, "were answered by children who had no idea where their parents were!"

CONCEIT

3068   **UNDERSTUDY IN LEADING ROLE**

A pushing young actor who was understudy in a popular play found his opportunity one night through the illness of his principal. He accordingly flooded his managerial and influential acquaintances with telegrams announcing: "I play So-and-So's part tonight." Except that the theatre was comparatively empty this breathless disclosure produced no result, other than a telegram in reply from the playwright to this effect: "Thanks for the warning."

3069   **MARINE PRIVATE AND NAVY COMMANDER—SPEED LIMIT**

During a recent drive on excessive speed at one of the larger naval installations in California, a Marine private stopped a military jeep for exceeding the speed limit and politely asked the driver, a Navy commander, for his operator's permit. The Marine proceeded to make out the traffic violation certificate.

"Private," the commander roared, "do you know who I am? I'm the executive officer of this base and I'm enroute to a golf engagement with your commanding officer, and this will undoubtedly make me late."

"I'm sorry, sir," the Marine replied, "but I'm writing as fast as I can."

3070   **THE WILDCAT AND A BUCKET OF WATER—STORIES ABOUT BRAVERY**

The men were swapping stories concerning their bravery.

"When I was logging up in Oregon," said one of them, "I saw a wildcat come right up to the skidder one day. It was a fierce beast, but with great presence of mind, I threw a bucket of water in its face and it slunk away."

Said a man sitting in the corner, "I can vouch for the truth of that story. A few minutes after that happened, I was coming down the side of the hill. I met this wildcat and, as is my habit, stopped to stroke its whiskers. Boy, those whiskers were wet!"

3071   **IT IS SAFER TO STAND UP**

In the days of Mussolini's higher prestige, it is said that he was once stranded in a small town due to the breaking down of his automobile. He went into a local cinema. When his picture appeared on the screen everyone rose but he remained seated. The manager of the theatre came forward, tapped him on the shoulder, whispering in his ear, "I feel the same way but you'd better stand up. It's safer."

3072   EX-PRESIDENT AND NUMBER OF AUTOMOBILES ROLLING BY

A newspaper correspondent visited Coolidge at Plymouth, watched the automobiles rolling by, and said:

"It must make you proud to see all these people coming by here, merely to look at you sitting on the porch. It shows that although you are an ex-President you are not forgotten. Just look at the number of those cars."

"Not as many as yesterday," replied Mr. Coolidge. "There were 163 then."

COURTSHIP

3073   DAUGHTER'S HAND—SEEKING

Suitor: "I am seeking your daughter's hand, sir. Have you any objections?"
Father: "None at all. Take the one that's always in my pocket."

3074   PRIVATE DETECTIVE'S REPORT

One of the powerful figures in Wall Street fell in love with an actress and for many months danced constant attendance upon her and squired her about in the fashionable circles of town. Deciding to marry her, he first prudently put a private detective to the job of looking into her antecedents in order to guard himself against any rash mistake. At last he received his agent's report. "Miss Blank enjoys an excellent reputation. Her past is spotless. Her associates have been irreproachable. The only breath of scandal is that, in recent months, she has been seen in the company of a businessman of doubtful reputation."

3075   THE MAN I MARRY—WANTED TV SET

A young coed looked dreamily at the ceiling and declared, "The man I marry must be an outstanding personality, be musical, tell new jokes, sing and dance, stay home, neither drink nor smoke, and shut up when I tell him to." Her caller arose, looked for his hat, and told her, "Lady, you don't want a husband, you want a television set."

3076   FAMILY'S OBJECTION TO SON'S GIRL

The family was objecting to their son's girl, insisting that he ought to be a little more particular about the company he kept.

"I'm sorry, Dad," said the boy, "but that's the best girl I can get with the car we've got."

3077   AN INVITATION FOR BREAKFAST—WILL I CALL YOU OR NUDGE YOU?

A young man, well-known for his cautious ways, met a girl at a cocktail lounge and they hit it off so well that he took her to a show. That went fine so he asked her to dinner. They enjoyed a leisurely dinner at a good hotel and followed that with a night club and dancing. Along toward midnight, they were having a snack at a table for two and he said to her, "You know, I've had a wonderful time ever since I met you this afternoon. I think we've hit it off swell together, don't you?"

"Sure," she agreed. "I've enjoyed it too."

"I'd like to have breakfast with you in the morning." And he looked at her eagerly. "May I?"

"Yes," she answered. "I'd like that very much."

"All right, what will I do, call you or nudge you?"

CREDIT AND DEBT

3078   NEW TECHNIQUE OF COLLECTION

A new technique of collection was practiced by the man who called up his debtor and demanded payment of a long outstanding account.

"I can't give it to you now," was the answer, as usual.

"Give it to me now," replied his ingenious creditor, "or I'll tell all your other creditors you've paid me."

3079   COLLECTION LETTER—RESULTS OF

A Nebraska newspaper declares the following collection letter produces excellent results:

"Dear Sir: A glance at the date of our original invoice will soon prove we've done more for you than even your own mother—*We've* carried you for 12 months."

3080   PALLBEARERS—DECEASED'S REQUEST FOR

This following note was found among the effects of a businessman after his death. He had long been known for his frequent lapses into bankruptcy.

"I hereby name the following six bankers to be my pallbearers. Since they have carried me for so long during my lifetime, they might as well finish the job now."

3081   NO DISGRACE—ONLY GOOD THING ABOUT POVERTY

Poverty is no disgrace—and that's the only good thing you can say about poverty.

DOCTORS

3082   TIRED OF CLIMBING UP AND DOWN THE DRAINPIPE

A very old lady fell down the stairs and broke her leg. The doctor put it in a cast and warned her not to walk up or down any stairs. Finally after six months the doctor announced that it was all right to remove the cast.

"Is it all right for me to climb the stairs now?" she asked.

"Yes," replied the doctor.

"Oh," she sighed, "I'm so glad. I'm tired of climbing up and down the drainpipe all the time!"

3083   LOVE LIFE OF ELDERLY MAN

A rather elderly gentleman had just had a medical checkup. The doctor smiled and said, "Well, I can't seem to find a thing wrong with you, but you aren't getting any younger, so I would recommend that you give up half of your love life."

After a long moment the patient said quietly, "Doctor, which half do you recommend I give up, thinking about it or talking about it?"

3084   STAIRS OR PILLS—TWO-AT-A-TIME

The condition of a man can best be judged by what he takes two-at-a-time—stairs or pills.

3085   DOCTOR'S FIRST PATIENT

Then there is the story of a young doctor who had just opened his office in a small town. He waited a few days for the arrival of his first patient—and finally one appeared. He was covered all over with a red, dangerous looking rash. The puzzled young doctor quickly consulted all his books but could find no help there.

At last he said to the patient, "Did you ever have this affliction before?"

Replied the patient, "Oh, sure, Doc. I've had it twice before."

"Well," diagnosed the doctor, "you have it again!"

3086   BOTHERED OBSTETRICIAN

It was a sweltering summer day, and the perspiring obstetrician was rushing frantically to examine all his patients before answering a summons from the hospital. "These hot August days getting you down, Doc?" asked one woman sympathetically.

"No," said the doctor, "it's not these hot August days that are bothering me— it's those cold nights last November."

3087   FIRST VISITOR—TELEPHONE INSTALLATION MAN

Young Dr. Anderson hung out his shingle for the first time on a Tuesday, but no patient showed up until Friday morning. When one came into the room, Dr. Anderson thought it advisable to impress him. He picked up his telephone and barked into it, "I have so many patients scheduled to visit me today that I am afraid I won't be able to get over to the hospital to perform that brain operation until six this evening." He hung up the receiver and turned to his visitor with a disarming smile. "What seems to be paining you, my good man?" he said.

"Nothing is paining me," said the bewildered visitor. "I have just come to hook up your phone, sir."

3088   CURE FOR DIZZINESS

A certain person came to a doctor and said, "Sir, when I awake from sleep I have a dizziness for half an hour, and then I feel all right."

"Well, get up after the half-hour," the physician replied.

3089   APPLYING FIRST AID KNOWLEDGE—TO SELF

An enthusiastic elderly lady once told a group of friends the wonderful opportunity she had had to apply the knowledge she had learned in her First Aid class. "It was simply wonderful," she exclaimed, "it was so fortunate that I had had the training. I was crossing Fifth Avenue at 57th street and heard a crash behind me. I turned around and saw a poor man who had been hit by a taxicab. He had a compound fracture of the leg, was bleeding terribly, was unconscious and seemed to have a fractured skull. Then all my First Aid came back to me; and I stooped right down and put my head between my legs to keep myself from fainting!"

3090   WOUNDED SOLDIER DURING WORLD WAR II

There were many persons who took First Aid courses during World War II. One elderly lady, determined to be of help, bent down solicitously over a wounded soldier whose head was swathed in bandages. "Are you wounded in the head, my boy?" she asked.

"No, ma'am," said the victim very feebly. "I was shot in the foot and the bandages slipped up."

DRINKING

3091   WAS I AT THE WAKE

"Finnegan," inquired Murphy, "is it true what they're saying about O'Brien's behavior at the wake last night?"

"Sure, it is so, Murphy. A disgrace to the Irish he was."

"And Mallory wanting to fight everybody, is that the truth?"

"Ah, Mallory was a crazy devil; he was worse than O'Brien."

"It's uncomplimentary reports I've been hearin' of Burke's deportment, too; was he guilty?"

"Burke passed out cold long before midnight. It's an embarrassment he'll never live down."

"I'm ashamed of our old friends, Finnegan. But tell me confidentially: was I there?"

3092   PLAYING GOLF WITH NIGHT CLUBS

Meeting her slightly tipsy husband at the door late one night, the wife demanded: "Well, what excuse do you have for coming home at this hour of the night?"

Replied the husband, "Well, my dear, I was playing golf with some of the office staff."

"What? At 2 a.m.?"

"We were using night clubs."

3093   SPEAKING FROM THE FLOOR

There is a new drink called "The Delegate." Two of them and you're speaking from the floor.

3094   LAST NIGHT—A FUNNY THING HAPPENED TO ME

"Did you get home all right last night?"

"I got home all right—but a funny thing happened to me. Just as I was turning the corner, someone stepped on my fingers."

3095   DRINKING COMPANIONS

For fear that one drink will be lonesome, take another to keep it company, and another to keep peace between them!

3096   NOW WHERE THE HELL'S THE CAT?

A favorite cat story involves two intrepid young husbands whose wives traipsed off for a summer vacation and left them in the city to keep house together as best they might.

One evening they purchased a four-pound sirloin steak, and left it on the kitchen table while they repaired to the library for a few libations. What with an extra dividend or two, they were weaving a bit when they re-entered the kitchen, but not too discombobulated to overlook the fact that their four-pound steak had disappeared.

A frantic search proved unproductive, but then one of the men noticed that a cat under the sink was licking his whiskers with an uncommonly satisfied air. "I'll bet," he exclaimed, "that cat has eaten our four-pound steak."

"One way to find out," said the other grimly. He seized the cat by the scruff of the neck and deposited it on the bathroom scale. Sure enough, it weighed exactly four pounds.

"Well," he announced triumphantly, "there's our four-pound steak all right. Now where the hell's the cat?"

3097   BRANDY FOR HIS FOREHEAD

A man who once cut his forehead, was advised to rub it vigorously with brandy. Some days later, when asked if he had done so, he replied, "I have tried several times, but can never get the glass higher than my mouth."

3098   HOW TO GET RID OF TWO EMPTY WHISKEY BOTTLES FOUND IN GARBAGE CAN

A prim and proper elderly lady found two empty whiskey bottles in her garbage can. It was an awful shock to her and she told her friend, "You can just imagine my embarrassment! I grabbed them out fast because I didn't want the garbage man to think I drink."

Asked her friend, "Well, what on earth did you do with them?"

She replied: "Oh, the preacher lives next door, so I put them in his can. Everybody knows he doesn't drink."

3099   DRUNKS ON BUS—LET'S GET OFF

Two rather inebriated men got on a bus. There happened to be a naval officer standing near the door, and one of the two drunks handed him two fares.

Greatly miffed, the man in blue said, "I'm a naval officer, not a conductor."

"Let's get off," called out the drunk to his companion, "We're on a battleship, not a bus!"

3100   THE WRONG BUS—STANDING STILL

A man who had imbibed too freely was very late getting home. His furious wife berated him for keeping her up. His excuse was that he had taken the wrong bus.

Said his wife, "That is easy to understand, considering the shape you're in, but how did you know you were on the wrong bus?"

Replied the flustered man, "Well, it seemed strange when it stood at one corner for a couple of hours, but what finally convinced me was the fact that people kept coming in and ordering hamburgers."

3101   SHRIMP COCKTAIL AS SMALL MARTINI

Taken to an expensive New York restaurant, an out-of-towner, a rough diamond, had the fanciest dinner of his life. He ordered a shrimp cocktail, but when it was placed before him, his face fell. "Hey, this is *seafood*," he protested. "I thought a shrimp cocktail meant a small martini."

3102   JAR FULL OF OLIVES—FELLOW FULL OF MARTINIS

A fellow came into a bar and ordered a martini. Before drinking it, he removed the olive and carefully put it into a small glass jar. Then he ordered another martini and did the same thing. After an hour, when he was full of martinis and the jar was full of olives he staggered out.

"Well," said a customer, "I never saw anything as peculiar as that!"

"What's so peculiar about it?" the bartender said. "His wife sent him out for a jar of olives."

EDUCATION

3103   AN AMERICAN UNIVERSITY AND CHINESE STUDENT

A Chinese student attending one of our universities wrote back to relatives to tell them about life in America. He said, "An American university is a vast athletic association; however, some studies are maintained for the benefit of the feeble-bodied."

3104   YOUNG SON'S REPORT CARD—FATHER LOOKING OVER

A father, looking over his young son's report card, had this to say, "One thing in your favor—with these grades, you couldn't possibly be cheating."

EMPLOYEES AND EMPLOYERS

3105   SHOP SUGGESTION BOX

A well-meaning employer desired to introduce a new spirit into his plant. He called his employees together, and said, "Whenever I come into the shop I want to see every man cheerfully at work. I am placing a box here and I should like anyone who has any suggestions as to how this may be brought about more efficiently to just put it in here."

The next day he saw a slip of paper in the box, took it out and looked at it. It said, "Take the rubber heels off your shoes."

3106   NEW DELIVERY BOY AND TURTLES IN ZOO

A store manager, irked by the behavior of his new delivery boy, asked him: "Been to the zoo yet?" The boy replied: "No sir." Said the manager: "Well, you really should. You'll get a big kick out of watching the turtles zip by!"

3107   BIGOTED BOSS ON SPELLING

Two secretaries were comparing bosses, and one said her boss was all right except that he was bigoted.

"Bigoted? How come?"

"Well, he thinks words can be spelled in only one way."

3108   REASON FOR HIGHER WAGES

"You are asking for pretty high wages for one who has so little experience," said the employer to an applicant.

"True," said the applicant, "but it is much harder work for me simply because I know so little about it."

3109   CLAPPING FOR OVERTIME

At the conclusion of a concert two ushers were applauding harder than anybody else. People seated nearby smiled appreciatively at the two music lovers—until one of them stopped applauding and the other one was heard to say, "Keep clapping, you dope. One more encore and we're on overtime."

3110   EMPLOYEE'S QUESTIONNAIRE—QUESTION AND ANSWER

Applying for a post as keeper at the Bronx Zoo, a burly Irishman came to the question, "What is rabies and what can you do about it?"

The applicant wrote: "Rabies is Jewish priests, and you can't do anything about it."

3111   NOTICE IN RESTAURANT

A sign was once noticed in a Hollywood restaurant which said: "Please don't insult our waiters. Customers we can get."

3112   STEADY EMPLOYMENT WHILE PAYING FOR SMASHED VASE

A very clumsy man who found it very difficult to find employment at long last found a job in a chinaware house. He had been at work only a few days when he smashed a large vase. He was immediately called to the manager's office and told that he would have to have the money deducted from his wages every week until the vase was paid for.

"How much did it cost?" asked the culprit.

"Three hundred dollars," said the manager.

"Oh, that's wonderful," he said, "I'm so happy. At last I've got a steady job!"

3113   ARRIVING LATE FOR WORK

One day a shipping clerk arrived late for work. He had one eye swollen shut, his left arm in a sling, and his clothes in tatters. "It's nine-thirty," the boss began, "and you were due at eight-thirty." Explained the employee, "I fell out of a four-story window...." Snorted the boss, "And it took you a whole hour?"

FAITH

3114   BIBLE STORY ABOUT RED SEA

Do you really believe the Bible story about the parting of the Red Sea for Moses and the Jews?" asked a congregant of his pastor.

The pastor smiled for a moment and replied: "I certainly do. If De Mille can do it, God can do it, too!"

3115   PRAYING FOR RAIN

During a particularly hot summer, a group of farmers met in their church to pray for rain. After the services a little girl asked her father if the people truly expected that it would rain. "Of course," replied her father, "otherwise, we wouldn't be here."

"But Daddy," she protested, "how come no one came to church with an umbrella?"

FRUSTRATION

3116   STARTING POINT—CONFUSED NATIVE GIVING DIRECTIONS

Then there's the native who gets sadly confused in giving directions and finally confesses: "Mister, if I was going to Harodsburg, I just wouldn't start from here."

3117   THREE MEN AND THEIR LAST WISHES

Three men traveling by boat in a heavy storm were told that the ship would sink within a half hour. Until then, they could have whatever they wished.

One asked for a strong drink and good food to satisfy his sensual desires.

The second asked to be left alone so he might contemplate in preparation for death.

The third, who loved life, himself, and his neighbors, asked: "Is there anyone here who can teach us how to live under water?"

3118   WRONG STRAW ON THE CAMEL'S BACK

At a zoo a man stood thoughtfully looking at a camel. Then he picked up a straw, placed it on the camel's back and waited. Nothing happened. Walking away, he muttered, "Wrong straw."

3119   NEW SON-IN-LAW CAN'T DRINK AND CAN'T PLAY CARDS

A man was complaining bitterly about his new son-in-law:
"He can't drink and he can't play cards." Consoled a friend:

"But that's the kind of son-in-law to have!" Replied the first:
"No, you don't understand at all. He can't play cards. But he plays. He can't drink—and he drinks."

GRATITUDE

3120   GIVING THANKS

Before Thanksgiving a Minnesota first-grade teacher asked her pupils to tell her what they had to be thankful for. "I am thankful," said one small boy, "that I am not a turkey."

3121   SEEING THE PALMS

New guest: "I don't know why they call this hotel The Palms. I haven't seen a palm near the place."
Old timer: "You'll see them before you go. They are reserved by the staff for the last day of your stay here."

3122   A LUMP OF SUGAR

One bitter cold day, Scotsman Harry Lauder played around the golf course. When he came off the green, he slipped something into the hand of his caddie, saying, "That's for a glass of hot whiskey, m'lad." The boy opened his hand and found a lump of sugar.

GOOD INTENTIONS

3123   BOY SCOUTS—GOOD DEEDS OF

Before the close of the meeting of the Boy Scouts in the parish hall, the pastor asked if each had done his good deed for the day.

Three little boys, who were friends, answered in unison that they had helped an old lady across the street.

"Did the three of you help the same old lady?" asked the pastor.

"Yes," came the reply from the same three.

Surprised, the pastor asked why it took all three to help the same old lady cross the street.

"Well," said the smallest of the trio, "cause she really didn't want to go!"

3124   SUNBATH—ON HOTEL DINING ROOM SKYLIGHT

At a small hotel on Miami Beach a young lady was on the roof taking a sun bath, wearing only a brief bikini. She noted that there were no tall buildings anywhere nearby. There was no way for anybody to see her so she decided to take off her suit and have a real sunbath. She did so, and lying on her stomach she was enjoying herself when she heard foot-steps approaching. She quickly grabbed her towel and looked up to see the hotel manager coming near. "Young lady," he said, "we do not allow nude sun bathing!"

"But," she explained, "there are no high buildings around."

"That I know," he said, "but you are lying on the skylight over the dining room."

3125   FLAGPOLE

I was attending an American Legion meeting in a small Pennsylvania town where the commander made up in directness what he might have lacked in following Robert's Rules of Order. A proposal that five feet be cut off the flagpole to give better clearance for the flag among the pine trees precipitated a heated discussion. Finally the commander rapped for order.

"Buddies," he said, "just so we'd finish the agenda, I cut five feet off that pole this afternoon. Now let's proceed."

GAMBLING

3126   LAST RITES FOR "LIVING DOLL"

His friends were always boasting about their winnings at the race track, and so Finnegan decided that he too would have a try at it. On his next day off, he drove out to Roosevelt Raceway. He put two dollars on each of the first four races and lost each time. He was a prudent man and made a fast decision; apparently, gambling was not his forte. He decided he had better leave before his week's wages were all gone.

As he was walking to the exit, he glanced toward the paddock and noticed a priest standing near one of the horses. He stopped and observed that the priest walked up close to the horse and rubbed his muzzle.

"A hunch, if ever I saw one," mused Finnegan. "The priest is blessing that horse and he's sure to be a winner!" He pointed to the horse and asked a stable boy its name.

"That's 'Living Doll' in the next race."

Finnegan dashed to the nearest window and put $25.00 on the nose! The race started, and Living Doll was the last one out of the gate. At the halfway mark, Living Doll trailed far behind the other horses. At the finish, the exhausted Living Doll had to be assisted to the line. Finnegan, dejected, left and started for the parking lot. There, he again saw the priest.

"Father, you let me down!"

Puzzled, the priest asked, "I? How?"

"Well, Father, as I was about to leave the track, I noticed you were blessing one of the horses. I thought that was a hunch and I put my last $25.00 on his nose. I suppose you know our horse came in last!"

"Son," the priest said, "I'm sorry if you misinterpreted my actions in the paddock. I was not blessing that horse; I was giving him the last rites."

3127   BAD LUCK AT RACE TRACK—TYCOONS DISCUSSING FRIEND'S

Two business tycoons were discussing a friend's bad luck at the race track. "It's funny," said one, "how lucky Herman is at cards and how he never wins a bet on the horses."

Replied the other, "There is really nothing peculiar about it. They just won't let him shuffle the horses."

HASTE

3128   PARAKEET UNDER CARPETING—HASTE OF FLOOR COVERING MAN

A family had had a beautiful new home built in suburbia and as soon as it was completed, they hurriedly moved in and employed a local man to lay wall-to-wall carpeting in the living room. The fellow worked in great haste and when he had completed his work, he noticed a small lump in the middle of the carpeting. He nervously felt in his pocket for his pack of cigarettes; they were gone. He quickly concluded that the pack had fallen from his pocket and was now under the rug so he furtively smoothed out the lump with his feet.

However, when he reached his truck, he was surprised to find that the cigarettes were on the car seat. And he was even more startled when the lady ran out of the house calling to him, "Have you seen anything of my parakeet?"

3129   WRONG GREETING CARDS—NINETY-NINE GIFTS ON THEIR WAY

In Salt Lake City a dilatory housewife bought a last-minute box of one hundred identical greeting cards, and, not even pausing to read the message, inscribed thereon, feverishly dispatched them to the ninety-nine relatives and acquaintances whose own greetings already were displayed on her piano top and mantel. Some days later she accidentally picked up the one card of her own she had not mailed, and read what it said in a state of shock: "This little card is just to say, 'A gift you'll love is on its way.'"

HECKLERS

3130   NAME-CALLING HECKLER—SPEAKER'S REQUEST TO

The political speaker found himself repeatedly interrupted by a heckler who shouted, "Liar!" again and again during his discourse. His patience exhausted, the speaker at last said, "If the gentleman will be good enough to tell us his name as well as his calling, we shall be pleased to hear from him."

3131   THE JACKASS—A HAUNTED UNITED STATES SENATOR AND HECKLER

A United States senator was regaling a banquet audience one evening when a heckler disturbed the smooth flow of his oratory. The senator frowned, and spoke as follows: "When I was a lad back on the farm, my dad once gave me for my birthday a wonderful little donkey. 'This is a mighty fine animal,' he told me, 'and I expect you to treat it accordingly. See that he's properly fed, curried down, and bedded. And always end up by locking the barn door.' Well, gentlemen, there came an evening, unfortunately, when I forgot to lock the barn door. The donkey walked out and got himself run over by a truck. My dad looked sadly at the carcass and said, 'Son, that animal's going to haunt you for the rest of your life,' and my dad sure hit the nail on the head."

The senator pointed to the heckler and concluded, "There sits that jackass now!"

HOSPITALITY

**3132   ATTENDING FRIEND'S WEDDING ANNIVERSARY IN APARTMENT
         HOUSE—HOW TO FIND HIM**

An Irishman, inviting a friend to his wedding anniversary, explained how to find him in the apartment house where he lived. "Come to the seventh floor," he said, "and where you see the letter D on the door, push the button with your elbow and when the door opens put your foot against it."

"Why do I have to use my elbow and my foot?" asked his friend.

"Why, for heaven's sake!" exclaimed the Irishman. "You're not coming empty-handed, are you?"

3133   IT HAPPENED TO MY SISTER—THE GENEROUS AMERICANO

A young Mexican fellow was telling his friend about the remarkable generosity of the American people. "The Americano is very generous. You can be a perfect stranger in a big city like Los Angeles and you may be walking down the street when all of a sudden an Americano will stop his big car next to the curb and ask you if you want to go for a ride. You may say yes and this generous Americano may ask you if you want to go to a fine restaurant for dinner and a show afterwards. When you have done this he may take you to a beautiful hotel where you will be his guest for the night. All these things he does for you and it doesn't cost you a cent."

The Mexican friend was astounded. "Did this happen to you?" he asked in amazement.

"No . . ." replied the first Mexican with simple directness, "but it happened to my sister."

3134   STRETCHING TIME—PEOPLE

Some people can stay longer in an hour than others can in a week.

3135   MANNERS AND DINNER GUESTS

President Coolidge had guests to dinner at the White House, friends from Vermont. They were worried about their table manners so decided to watch Cal and do whatever he did. When Cal poured his coffee into his saucer, they did the same; when he added sugar and cream to the coffee in the saucer, they did the same. Then the President placed the saucer of coffee on the floor for the cat.

INGENUITY

3136   STUCK IN THE TOBACCO ROAD REGION

Not all inhabitants of the Tobacco Road region of Georgia are as indigent as the Lester family. Witness the case of the motorist who had become bogged down in the sticky clay of an unpaved Georgia road, and had paid $10 to be pulled out by a Georgia cracker with a team of mules. "I should think," said the motorist, just about to get into his car to continue, "that you would be pulling people out of this stuff day and night."

"Nope," drawled the mule driver, "at night's when we tote the water for the roads."

3137   A SHOE FIT FOR A QUEEN

"This," said the manager of the store, "is an inferior grade of shoe. I'm an honorable business man and I refuse to pass it off as anything better. Put it in the window and mark it—'A Shoe Fit for a Queen.' A queen does not have to do much walking."

3138   AUTOMOBILE POWERED BY ELECTRICITY

A grimly determined inventor, undaunted by a series of grisly failures, kept working away on a long-range automobile powered by electricity instead of gasoline. He dashed triumphantly into the Explorers' Club in New York one evening, and cried, "I've done it! All the way from Mexico City without a single mishap!" Pressed for a report on the cost of the trip, the inventor replied, "Exactly $3955.88—three dollars for electricity and $3952.88 for the extension cord."

3139   TEACHING MAN—THE TALKING, READING AND WRITING DOG

Craziest story of the month concerns a college student who couldn't live on the scale to which he was accustomed on the modest allowance doled out to him by his parents. Desperate to wangle a bonus from his father, he bethought himself of a dachshund named Man that was the old man's pride and joy, and wired him: "There's a professor here who can teach Man to talk for two hundred dollars cash. What do you say?" Papa said yes, and wired the two hundred. Convinced he was now launched on a sure thing, the rascally son squandered the two hundred, then wired Papa again: "For three hundred dollars more, the professor guarantees to teach Man how to read and write."

"Wonderful," enthused the father—and produced the cash once more.

Papa was waiting at the station when his son came home for spring vacation. "Where's Man?" he cried. "I can't wait to see him talk, read and write."

"I have a disappointment, Father," said the student. "Yesterday, I said to Man, 'Tomorrow's the day we go home and see the family. Won't that be great?' Man answered, 'I wonder if your mother's found out yet that your father's carrying on with that cheap blonde at the nightclub. What a ball we'll have dropping *that* into the open.' Well, Father, when I heard Man go on like that, I felt there was only one thing to do. I shot him."

Papa reflected for just a moment, then spoke as follows: "My boy, there is only one more thing I wish to know. Are you sure that blank-blank dog is dead?"

LAZINESS

3140   RANCHER AND HIS HORSE

When a young man and his wife, city born and bred, first moved to an isolated part of Wyoming, a neighboring rancher gave generously of his time and experience in helping them get started. They noticed that he invariably hopped on his horse to do even the shortest errand. One day, when he mounted to ride no more than 30 feet, my husband said, "Don't you *ever* walk?"

"Son," the rancher replied seriously, "if the good Lord had wanted me to walk, he'd have given me four legs!"

3141   THE EASY WAY OUT

An old rancher in eastern Kansas was hoeing his corn in the hot summer sun. "Why don't you hitch the team up and plow those weeds out with a cultivator?" his more energetic brother-in-law asked.

"Oh, I dunno," the rancher replied, "it's so easy to quit this way!"

JUSTICE AND THE LAW

3142   VERDICT—"NOT GUILTY"

A community was shocked to learn that a murder in its midst had been committed by one of the town's most popular and well-liked men. And realizing that the evidence against him was conclusive, the man entered a plea of guilty. There seemed to be no way of saving him from the electric chair.

However, the jurors were all friends of his and they were determined to save him in spite of his plea of guilty. So, at the conclusion of the case, they were asked to give their verdict, which was "Not guilty."

"Now how in the world," said the judge, "can you bring in such a verdict when the defendant pleaded guilty?"

"Well, your Honor," said the foreman of the jury, "the defendant is such a notorious liar that we can't believe him, even under oath!"

3143   QUESTION OF ARSON

There is a well-known insurance executive who swears it is true that the same day a merchant took out fire insurance, his store and all its contents were burned to the ground. When the storekeeper filed an insurance claim, the company, suspecting arson but unable to prove it, wrote the man as follows:

"Dear Sir: You insured your store and its contents against fire at 10:30 A.M. The official report indicates that the fire did not break out until 4 P.M. the same day. Will you be good enough to explain the delay?"

3144   BEHAVIOR OF THE FARMER'S WIFE

An insurance salesman was getting nowhere in his efforts to sell a policy to a farmer. "Look at it this way," he said finally. "How would your wife carry on if you should die?"

"Well," answered the farmer reasonably, "I don't reckon that's any concern o'mine—so long as she behaves herself while I'm alive."

3145   TRADE OF LAWYERS

It is the trade of lawyers to question everything, yield nothing, and to talk by the hour.

3146   PROVING LAWYER IS A CRIMINAL

A stranger, arriving in a small New England town, approached the first native he saw and asked:

"Have you a criminal lawyer in this town?"

"Well," replied the native cautiously, "we think we have but so far we can't prove it on him."

LOGIC

3147   IMPRESSION OF A FAMOUS LANDMARK

That celebrated landmark of Paris, the Eiffel Tower, has been the butt of much abuse in its time; Balzac is said to have fled screaming from the sight of it, saying that he could not endure its colossal vulgarity.

William Morris, the English poet, appears to have shared a somewhat similar view. During a long stay in Paris he very nearly cloistered himself in the restaurants of the Eiffel Tower, not only taking all his meals but even doing much of his writing there.

"You're certainly impressed by the Tower," someone once remarked to him.

"Impressed!" said Morris, "I stay here because it's the only place in Paris where I can avoid seeing the damn thing!"

3148   TASTELESS, SMALL TOMATOES—BUYING

A vacationer in Maine stopped at a wayside stand to buy some tomatoes. The customer looked through some baskets and then commented that they were rather small. The proprietor heartily agreed.

A day or two later, the customer returned and mentioned that the tomatoes had been rather tasteless. The elderly gentleman nodded and said, "So it was lucky they were small, wasn't it?"

3149   THE HAY FORK AND THE DOG—THE OTHER END OF

If your opponent complains that your tactics are unfair, the answer is to make clear that he initiated the rough play.

A farmer was returning from his field with a hay fork on his shoulder. As he was passing the house of a neighbor a vicious bulldog ran out and attacked him. The farmer drew his fork and speared the dog, pinning him to the ground.

Just then the owner of the dog came out, angrily shouting: "Now you have killed my valuable dog. You will pay for this. I'm going to have the law on you."

"I'm sorry," said the farmer, "but I had to do it."

"You didn't have to do it either. Why didn't you come at him with the other end of that fork?"

The farmer replied: "Why didn't he come at me with the other end?"

3150   DINOSAUR BONES—AGE OF

A tourist was visiting New Mexico. While gazing at the dinosaur bones that were everywhere, he met an old Indian who acted as an unofficial guide.

"How old are those bones?" asked the tourist.

Exactly one hundred million and three years old," was the Indian's reply.

"How can you be so definite?" inquired the tourist.

"Oh, a geologist told me they were one hundred million years old," replied the Indian, "and that was exactly three years ago."

3151   SHAKESPEARE OR BACON—TURNING OVER IN GRAVE

In a North of England town recently, a company of local amateurs produced *Hamlet,* and the following account of the proceedings appeared in the local paper next morning: "Last night all the fashionable and elite of our town gathered to witness a performance of *Hamlet* at the Town Hall. There has been considerable discussion in the press as to whether the play was written by Shakespeare or Bacon. All doubt can now be set at rest. Let their graves be opened; the one who turned over last night is the author."

LOYALTY

3152   REAL FRIENDS—HUSBAND SPENDING THE NIGHT WITH

Loyalty sometimes proves embarrassing. A case in point is that of the wife whose husband was unusually late, who wired to five of his friends, "Jack not home. Is he spending the night with you?" The unfortunate Jack arrived home shortly afterwards, and was followed by five telegrams all saying, "Yes."

3153   MONEY AND DOGS—THINKING ABOUT

A young boy had tried very hard to get his father to buy him a dog. Finally relenting, the father put this question to him: "If I gave you two hundred dollars, would you buy two one-hundred-dollar dogs, one two-hundred-dollar dog, or one one-hundred-dollar dog and put one hundred dollars in the bank for a rainy day?"

The boy thought for a long moment, "Well, if you leave it to me, I'd buy two hundred one-dollar dogs."

3154   THE ART OF HUNTING

There was once a cowboy from one of the many western dude ranches who spent his day off doing a little hunting. Sighting an eagle, he took careful aim and brought the bird down. He scurried down the cliff, took the bird, and as he looked up noticed one of the customers of his dude ranch looking at him.

The Easterner watched him for a moment, and then hesitantly offered the following words of advice:

"Excuse me, but I have been watching you. You know you should have saved that shot. Why, the fall alone would have killed that eagle."

3155   ASLEEP IN BED

I was asking motherly questions of our son, home on leave after completing boot camp. "How was your bed?" I asked. "Was it comfortable?"

He paused thoughtfully, then said, "I guess I don't know. Every time I was in it, I was asleep."

3156   WHY THE CAPTAIN ALWAYS GOES DOWN WITH HIS SHIP

A Navy recruit lost his rifle on the firing range. When told that he'd have to pay for it, he protested: "Suppose I was driving a Navy jeep and somebody stole it. Would I have to pay for that, too?" He was informed that he would have to pay for all government property he lost.

"Now," the recruit said, "I know why the captain always goes down with his ship."

3157   AND A LITTLE CHILD SHALL LEAD THEM—ON A DAMNED BIG HORSE

A green young lieutenant was assigned to a new detachment. He was a very small and helpless looking individual, and when he first appeared before his company there were many audible comments made about his apparent ineptness. From the rear of the ranks a voice boomed, "And a little child shall lead them." There was a roar of laughter.

Seemingly undisturbed the lieutenant finished the business of the day. Next day there appeared a notice on the bulletin board: "Company A will take a 25-mile hike today with full packs. And a little child shall lead them . . . on a damned big horse."

LUCK

3158   BONUS RAFFLE—DRAWING NUMBERED SLIPS FROM A HAT

In the Longacre sector of Manhattan, a group of well-known theatrical personalities invaded a dilapidated boarding house last Christmas season, intent upon bringing cheer to an old friend, proverbially unlucky, who once had been the most glittering star of them all. Knowing that he was too proud to accept anything more than a token gift, they rigged up a bonus raffle for a thousand dollars. The old actor was told that they would all draw slips from a hat, and that the man who drew the number four would win the thousand. To make sure the actor would win, a number four had been written on *every* slip in the hat.

They all drew slips and looked at them. The conspirators, of course, crumpled their slips and slipped them into their pockets, then waited for the actor to shout, "I've won!" But he never opened his mouth. Finally, they asked him what number he had drawn from the inside of the hat. He answered glumly, "Six and seven-eighths."

3159   POOR AND UNHAPPY—GETTING USED TO IT

A fortune teller faced a particularly apprehensive and hopeful looking customer. After careful study and thought the fortune teller said, "You'll be poor and unhappy until you are forty."

Replied the client hopefully, "Then what?"

"Then you'll get used to it."

3160   DRILLING FOR WATER

A motorist pulled up at a filling station in Texas. He noted that the gas attendant, an elderly man, looked very sad. The motorist remarked: "Everything certainly looks very dry."

"Yes."

"When did it rain last?"

"About three years ago."

"That must be so hard on the ranches around here," said the motorist sympathetically.

The man shook his head slowly: "I don't know what is to become of us. We have sunk thousands of wells drilling for water. And what comes up? Oil!"

MARRIAGE

3161   OUT AND INTO THE FRYING PAN

A lovely lady from the Social Register married a successful writer some years ago, but finally had to divorce him. Writers evidently were too temperamental and unpredictable, she complained, and she no longer could put up with this one's quirks and peccadillos.

What did she do then, however, but fall in love with another famous man of letters! The ex-husband read the wedding announcement in a European paper, and sent his former bride this cable: "Heartiest congratulations and best wishes. (Signed) Frying Pan."

3162   IN THE CASE OF THE FIRST CHILD—BUT NEVER AFTERWARDS

A gentleman whose wife was delivered of a boy six months after marriage, asked a physician the reason for this. "Make yourself easy," said the latter, "this often happens in the case of the first child, but never afterwards."

3163 HUSBAND'S STRONG WILL—WIFE'S KIND OF WILL

A young man, contemplating marriage, was almost shocked out of his future state by overhearing the following conversation:

Several young women, discussing their husbands, were talking of their men's vices and how they had succeeded in curing them.

"Incidentally," said one of them to a very pretty young thing standing by, "I hear that John has given up smoking. He used to smoke a great deal. That must have taken a strong will."

In contrast to her frail prettiness, the young woman was heard to say, "It certainly did. But that's the kind of will I've got."

3164 AMERICA—HOME OF THE BRAVE

"A large number of divorces indicate that America is still the land of the free," someone observed.

"Yes," said his friend, "but the steady level of the marriage rate shows that it's still the home of the brave."

3165 LOCKED OUT—HONEY, OH HONEY; MADAM, THIS IS NOT A BEEHIVE, IT'S A BATHROOM

While on her honeymoon the young bride had gone out alone one afternoon to make a few purchases. Coming back to the hotel where she had been accustomed to trustfully following her husband's guidance, she got off the elevator at the wrong floor. She went down the corridor until she reached what she supposed to be the door of her room. Finding it locked and having no key with her she knocked upon it and called out softly, "Honey, oh Honey."

There was no response. After a while she knocked again, calling somewhat more loudly, "Honey, oh Honey."

When this had occurred a number of times, a blatant male voice roared out from within, saying, "Madam, this is not a beehive, it's a bathroom."

3166 PLAYING HUSBAND—WITH A SPEAKING PART

An ambitious Yale student got a job with a summer theatre and came home to report triumphantly, "I've snagged my first part! Next week I'm going to play a husband who's been married for thirty years!" "Good start," approved his father. "Just you stick to it, and you'll get a speaking part yet!"

3167 DRESSED IN TUXEDO AND BLACK TIE—BY UNDERTAKER

Caspar Milquetoast had been advised by his psychiatrist to go home and assert himself. "Don't let your wife bully you any more. Go home and show her who's the boss."

So, the timid soul went home, banged the door shut, and said in a loud voice, "Now get this! From now on, I'm the boss in this joint, and I'm giving the orders and you're obeying them. Now get busy and get my supper on the table right away and after that, lay out my clothes because I'm going out tonight—alone—in my tuxedo. And do you know who's going to dress me in my tuxedo and black tie?"

"Yes, dear," replied the wife softly, "the undertaker."

3168   RANCHER—CALLING THE SHOTS

A young rancher, close-mouthed but with a terrible temper, got married. After the wedding they rode to his ranch in a small carriage, pulled by a mare. After a while the mare stumbled.

They rode along for a while more and the mare stumbled again. "That's twice," the rancher said. When the mare stumbled for the third time, the rancher cried, "That's three times."

He stopped the buggy, got out his gun and shot the mare dead.

His wife, angry because he had shot a good mare, bawled him out. He listened until she had finished and said, "That's once!"

3169   HUGGINS TALENTS—I MARRIED HIS WIDOW

Two friends stood talking on the street: "The greatest person who ever lived was Huggins—brilliant, broadminded, tolerant, generous, temperate; yet he died with his talents unsuspected."

"How did you manage to find out about him?" asked the listener.

Replied the first, "I married his widow."

3170   SEAT OF TROUSERS—HOLE IN

The young bride was in tears when her husband arrived home from his day of work. "Oh, I feel terrible," she cried. "I was pressing your best suit and I burnt a hole in the seat of the trousers."

Soothed her husband, "Don't worry about it. I happen to have another pair of pants to that suit."

Sniffling, she replied, "Yes, I know. And wasn't that lucky because I was able to use them to patch the hole."

3171   DIVULGING DIFFERENCE IN AGE FOR BETTER CHANCE OF MARRIAGE

A seasoned Broadway actor confided to his best friend, "I'm almost sixty-five years old, have saved half a million and have fallen madly in love with a young blond. Do you think I'd have a better chance of marrying her if I told her I'm only fifty?" Replied his pal, "Frankly, I think you would have a better chance if you told her you're eighty!"

3172   WIFE—THE BREAKING POINT OF

A wife whose husband spent most of his evenings away from home at committees, or playing cards, finally reached her breaking point one night when he departed with his customary words, "Goodnight, mother of three." This time she retorted, "And goodnight, father of none." He now spends his evenings at home!

3173   A BIRTHDAY PRESENT—SURPRISE FOR WIFE

A famous author was autographing copies of his new book in a New York bookstore. He was so pleased when a gentleman not only brought up his new book, but copies of his two previous ones as well. Remarked the purchaser, "My wife likes your stuff so I thought I'd give her these signed copies for a birthday present." Smiled the author, "A surprise?"

"I'll say," agreed the customer. "She's expecting a Cadillac."

3174   WANTED A BOY

A frail and henpecked husband was terribly disappointed when his wife gave birth to a baby daughter. He confided to a friend, "I was hoping for a boy to help me with the housework."

3175   DANCING IN THE NIGHT—DIFFERENCE BETWEEN MARRIED MAN AND UNMARRIED MAN

The difference between a married man and an unmarried man is that when a bachelor walks the floor with a baby, he's dancing.

3176   NEWLYWEDS GRIPE ABOUT CHORES

Overheard in a supermarket, one newlywed to another: "Marriage is really a grind. You wash dishes, make beds—then two weeks later you have to do it all over again."

3177   WALKING IT OFF—GRANDPA CARTWELL

Grandpa Cartwell was celebrating his 100th birthday and everybody complimented him on how athletic and well preserved he appeared. "I will tell you the secret of my success," he cackled. "My wife and I were married 75 years ago. On our wedding night we made a solemn pledge that whenever we had a fight, the one who was proved wrong would go out and take a walk. Gentlemen, I have been in the open air practically continuously for 75 years."

3178   THE HOMESICK GUY—WAITRESS SUBSTITUTING FOR NAGGING WIFE

A man who looked as if he had lost his last friend entered a restaurant one morning and sat down at a table. Said he to the waitress: "Bring me two eggs fried hard, a slice of toast burned to a cinder, and a cup of very weak coffee."

"Will you repeat that order," said the mystified waitress.

He did, and in a few minutes she brought the order. As she set it in front of him, she asked: "Anything else, sir?"

"Yes," he answered, "now sit down and nag me; I'm homesick."

3179   BLUSHING BRIDE AS PORTER

"Henry, darling," said the blushing bride, as the honeymooners drove up to the portico of the St. Regis, "let's try to convince all the hangers-on in the lobby that we've been married for ages."

"Okay, my love," said Henry dubiously, "but do you think you can carry four suitcases?"

3180   HOW TO BECOME A MILLIONAIRE

A millionaire, asked the reason for his success, said, "I never hesitate to give full credit to my wife."

"And how did she help?"

"Frankly," said the millionaire, "I was curious to see if there was any income she couldn't live beyond."

3181   STRANGE VOTING BOOTH

The jealous husband returned home from a business trip a day early and, discovering a strange coat in the front closet, stormed into the living room with the accusation that there was another man in the apartment.

"Where is he?" the husband demanded, as he stalked from room to room, searching.

The wife insisted, "You're mistaken, dear, that coat must have been left by one of your friends the last time you threw a poker party. Since you've been gone, I haven't seen or even looked at another man."

The husband searched through the entire apartment, and finding no one decided his wife must be telling the truth. Apologizing for his display of temper, he then went to the bathroom to wash up. He was running water in the basin when he noticed that the shower curtain was pulled close. Rather strange, he thought. He ripped the curtain open and sure enough—there stood a strange man. But before the astonished husband could utter a word, the man jerked the curtain closed again, saying: "Please! I haven't finished voting yet."

3182   THE LEAPING HUSBAND

A wife and her husband were sound asleep. At about 2 a.m. the wife dreamed she was in another man's arms. Then she dreamed she saw her husband coming toward her. In her sleep she shrieked out loud, "My husband!"

Her husband beside her was awakened by her cry and leaped out the window!

3183   MAN OF HIS WORD

A friend who usually takes a bus to work overslept one morning and decided to drive. As he opened the garage door he saw that the rear wall—the one his wife smashed when she stepped on the gas pedal instead of the brake—had not been repaired. My friend, a man of his word who expects the same virtue in others, strode back into the house and telephoned the carpenter. "You said that you would have it fixed by noon yesterday," he stormed.

"Let me ask you one question," said the carpenter quietly; "Did your wife drive the car in the afternoon?"

3184   FOUR BUSINESS MOGULS ROUGHING IT

Four staid, successful Minneapolis business moguls invested jointly in a hunting lodge deep in the Northern woods, and thither they were wont to repair for a fortnight twice a year. "Roughing it is what we want," they would tell their wives, "no hot water, no modern conveniences—and above all, no women!"

One September the four deserted ladies decided to surprise their husbands and followed them to their woodland lair. They were stopped at the gate, however, by a wizened old guide. "You gals better beat it quick if you know what's good for you," he advised. "This time these fellows brought their wives with them!"

3185   BEWARE PLAYBOY

A New York playboy was in a local barbershop, and the manicure girl was very beautiful. The playboy couldn't keep his eyes off of her and at last suggested dinner and a show that evening.

"I really don't think I ought to," said the girl quietly, "I'm married."

Suggested the playboy, "Ask your husband. Maybe he wouldn't mind."

"Ask him yourself," said the girl. "He's shaving you."

3186   HUSBAND'S EXPLANATION FOR PUSHING WIFE OUT OF BED

A young officer in a parachute division was home on leave for the first time since his honeymoon. In the middle of the night, his bride awoke to find herself without covers. Then, suddenly, she was pushed out of bed with such force that she crashed against the wall. Annoyed and bruised, she shook her husband awake and demanded the reason.

"You wouldn't jump, so I had to push you," mumbled the bridgegroom, and went calmly back to sleep.

MILITARY

3187   WAITING FOR THE PAINT TO DRY

The chief warrant officer was particularly proud of the cleanliness of the ship's engine room. The enlisted men under him lacked his enthusiasm; they had to do the work.

One day a "white hat" had just finished putting what seemed to be the ninety-ninth coat of high gloss enamel on the reduction-gear housing. He was sitting admiring his handiwork when the chief appeared and demanded to know why he was loafing.

"I'm waiting for the paint to dry," the sailor said, "so I can start scrubbing it."

3188   THREE SACRED RULES OF THE SERVICE

A three-year hitch in the army enabled one observant recruit to boil everything down to three sacred rules: *One*: If it moves, salute it. *Two*: If it doesn't move, pick it up. *Three*: If it's too big to pick up, paint it.

3189   INEXPERIENCED LIEUTENANT LOOKING FOR FOXHOLE

A Marine lieutenant, straight from the platoon-leader course at Quantico, took command of a battle-experienced platoon on the main line of resistance in Korea. As his first night approached and his platoon began to dig their foxholes, the green lieutenant asked his platoon sergeant, "Sergeant, where is my foxhole?"

"Lieutenant," replied the sergeant, "You're standing in it. You just haven't thrown the dirt out, sir!"

3190   BAD BOUNCE ON AIRSTRIP

A fighter wing was receiving the first of its new F-100D Super Sabre jet fighters, being delivered by none other than the air division commander himself, a young brigadier general. All the pilots had gathered on the flight line to watch the landing, and as luck would have it the general made a terrific bounce. "Boy," exclaimed one of our newer second lieutenants, "look at him bounce!"

The squadron operations officer, an old-timer, told the lieutenant firmly, "Son, when lieutenants land like that, they bounce. When generals land like that, you'll find it more profitable to say, 'Kind of gusty out there today!' "

3191   ARTIST'S VERSION OF A PERFECT FEMALE

Glancing through a copy of *Stars and Stripes*, a serviceman found an article on the ideal woman. "A group of artists," he read to the barracks in general, "have created the perfect female. They have taken Brigitte Bardot's nose, Rita Hayworth's mouth, Lana Turner's eyes and Grace Kelly's chin."

"I shore would like to have what they throwed away," drawled a voice from the corner."

MONEY AND PRICES

3192   PAPER NAPKIN—THE LIGHT TOUCH OF

A cashier at a restaurant was asked why he kept a paper napkin next to the cash box. "Whenever a customer walks off without his change," he explained, "I tap the counter with it as hard as I can."

3193   MIXED GREENS—VALUE OF

Mixed greens are good for you—especially the fives, tens, and twenties.

3194   INVISIBLE ASSETS

The reason it is so difficult to make both ends meet is that just when you are about to do so, some fools come along and move the ends.

3195   POOR—MISFORTUNE OF MANY

One of the strangest things about life is that the poor, who need money the most, are the very ones that never have it!   *Finley Peter Dunne*

3196   THE THRIFTY GOLFER—LAST GOLF BALL OF

I wouldn't say that John Brown is cheap, you understand. But yesterday he lost his first golf ball in ten years. The string broke.

3197   PRICE OF A HAIRCUT

Customer: "Does a man with as little hair as I've got have to pay full price to have it cut?"

Barber: "Yes, and sometimes more. We usually charge double when we have to hunt for the hair."

3198 CAR OWNER'S SURPRISE

The value of specialized training is exemplified in this little episode.

The car simply would not run. The mechanic was called in, lifted the hood, reached inside, gave a twist of the wrist to a little mechanism—and all was well.

"What do I owe you?"

"One dollar and ten cents," said the mechanic.

"Great Heavens!" remonstrated the car owner. "It seems like an awful lot for just twisting a little gadget. How do you itemize it?"

"Well," said the mechanic, "for twisting the little gadget—10¢. For knowing which little gadget to twist—$1.00."

3199 REASON FOR HIGH PRICE OF APPLES

A woman shopping in a grocery store was shocked by the high price of apples. "Yes, they're high, all right, ma'am. But that is because they are scarce."

"But," protested the woman, "just this morning I read in the paper that there was such a bumper crop of apples they're rotting on the trees."

"That's just it," replied the clerk. "That's why they're scarce. It just doesn't pay to pick them."

3200 LENDING A HELPING HAND

Somebody is always ready to lend a helping hand—if you have any trouble opening your pocketbook.

3201 BURIED IN A CADILLAC

A group of friends of a departed colleague were discussing the funeral of their friend. "Oh, it was quite an event," said one. "And I understand it cost fifty-eight hundred dollars."

"Good grief!" exclaimed another. "Five bills more and he could have been buried in a Cadillac."

3202 POSTDATED CHECK—VALUE OF

Driving through a New England state a motorist knocked down a calf which was crossing the road. Noticing a farmhouse down the road, he stopped there to report the accident. The owner also owned the calf, and the motorist immediately apologized and asked how much the animal was worth.

Replied the farmer slowly, "Well, it's worth $35 now. But in six years it would have been worth $250!"

The motorist sat down, took out his checkbook and after writing a check, handed it to the farmer. "And there you are," he said. "That's a postdated check for $250."

3203   ONE LESS IN THE FAMILY

A harried wife who was figuring out her expenses said to her husband and children: "Well, I worked out a budget. But one of us will have to go."

3204   ASTRONAUT'S THOUGHTS ABOUT THE LOWEST BIDDER

A space-agency psychologist asked one of the astronauts what he was thinking about as he strapped himself into his craft atop the rocket which was to hurl him into space.

"All I keep thinking," he replied, "is that everything that makes this thing go was supplied by the lowest bidder!"

MOTHERS AND FATHERS

3205   BOY SCOUT AND HIDDEN UMBRELLA

During the preliminary inspection at a Boy Scout camp near Hazleton, Pennsylvania, the director found a large umbrella hidden in the bedroll of a tiny scouter. Obviously not one of the items of equipment listed, the director asked the lad to explain. The tenderfoot did so neatly by asking: "Sir, did you ever have a mother?"

3206   BOB'S NOSE DISCOVERED BY MOTHER

"It was mother who discovered my nose," Bob Hope once remarked. "She looked at it, turned to father and said, 'William, call the doctor and tell him there's been a terrible mistake. They have taken the baby and left the stork.'"

3207   CENSUS MAN—NUMBERS OF CHILDREN

A census man going his rounds and he knocked on one door to learn who lived behind it. He asked the woman who opened it how many children she had. She said: "Well, there's Willie and Horace and Esther..."

The census taker interrupted: "Never mind names. I just wanted numbers."

Replied the indignant mother: "They haven't got numbers; every one of them's got names."

3208   CAUTIOUS MOTHER—WHAT TO DO WHEN BABY CUTS FIRST TOOTH

There was once an extra cautious mother who always wore a guaze mask when coming near her baby, and she expected all her visitors to do the same. Several people tried to tell her that this was carrying things a bit too far, but she would hear none of it. She was frantic in her attempts to maintain her child's health.

However one day the mother mentioned that she thought her baby was beginning to cut a tooth and wished she could in some way find out about it. A friend of hers with more experience said, "Why, just put your finger in his mouth and . . ."

There was such a horrified expression on the mother's face that the friend quickly added, "Of course, boil your finger first."

3209   A JOB WELL DONE

A mother of thirteen children was asked, "How in the world do you have time to care for so many?"

"Well," the mother replied, "when I had only one child it took all my time, so what more can thirteen do?"

3210   A BRIGHT MISUNDERSTANDING

Exclaimed a mother reading a letter from her son in the Army: "They have promoted our Henry for being the only one who had the nerve to hit that tough top sergeant. They've made Henry a court marshal!"

3211   MISTAKEN FATHERHOOD

Getting on a trolley car, a kindergarten teacher sat down next to a man who appeared familiar to her. Smiling pleasantly, she turned as if to speak to him. Noticing his lack of response, she realized her error, and said, "Oh, excuse me. I mistook you for someone else. I thought you were the father of two of my children."

He got out at the next corner.

3212   DUCK HUNTING—FATHER AND SON

A father, very anxious to impress his young son, told him what a great shot he was. And to prove his point he took his boy out duck hunting with him one day. The ducks were scarce but finally one solitary duck flew overhead and the father took careful aim and fired. The duck kept right on going. Turning to the son he said: "Son, you've just witnessed a miracle. There flies a dead duck."

MOTIVATION

3213 LANDLORD AS GOOD SAMARITAN

A housewife answered her doorbell to find a man taking up a collection for an impoverished widow down the block. Not only was she short of clothes and victuals, he said, but she was about to be thrown out into the bitter cold because she owed four months' rent.

"Well, at least she's lucky to have found such a good Samaritan," philosophized the housewife. "Who are you?"

"I," said the good Samaritan, "am her landlord."

3214 SPECIES OF CREATURES

There are three species of creatures who, when they seem coming are going, when they seem going they come: diplomats, women, and crabs.

OPPORTUNITY

3215 TURNING BACK THE CALENDAR—TO MAKE A FORTUNE

A man in Glencoe bought a million 1942 calendars for a penny apiece. "What on earth are you going to do with them?" he was asked. "It's rather a long chance, I admit," he said, "but, oh boy, if 1942 ever comes back, I'll make a fortune."

3216 SECRET OF SUCCESS—ON THE MOVE

A very ambitious young man asked a successful merchant the secret of his great success. "There is no secret," said the merchant, "Just jump at your opportunity."

"But," said the young man, "how can I tell when my opportunity is coming?"

"You can't. You have to keep jumping."

3217   WHAT GLORY—AT FUND-RAISING RALLY

The speaker at a fund-raising rally said, "Will all those who wish to contribute $100 please stand up"—then in an aside to the bandleader, he said, "Quick, play 'The Star Spangled Banner!' "

3218   I WONDER WHAT THAT KNOCKING WAS?—IT WASN'T OPPORTUNITY

A young man-about-town took a glamorous girl out one night. They were driving down a moonlit country lane when the engine suddenly coughed and the car came to a halt. "That's funny," said the young man. "I wonder what that knocking was?"

"Well, I can tell you one thing for sure," the girl answered icily, "It wasn't opportunity."

3219   TO GROW BIGGER—SECRET OF SUCCESS

A circus manager appraised the little man who had applied for the job of wild-animal trainer, then asked, "Aren't you kind of small for this work?"

"That's the secret of my success," replied the applicant. "The animals keep waiting for me to grow bigger."

3220   WARNING TO NEIGHBOR—BY PRINCETON GRADUATE

When a Princeton graduate inherited a cattle ranch out west, he soon discovered that the ornery galoot on an adjoining ranch was rustling his stock. "Be careful," he was warned. "That old crook is as liable as not to drill a coupla holes in your hide." So this is the warning note that the Princeton grad typed out: "Dear Sir: I'd appreciate it if you'd stop leaving your hot branding irons out where my fool cattle can sit down on them."

3221   CLASSIFIED AD—FAIR EXCHANGE OF BOTTLES

Classified ad quoted verbatim from the London *Times*: "Attention ship-in-bottle makers: I offer you my services gratis. I will accept full bottles of amontillado sherry, or Haig and Haig whiskey, and return them ready for insertion of ship. Prompt, conscientious work guaranteed. Address Box DSK."

3222   WANTED HARVARD MAN OR EQUIVALENT—SIMPLE ARITHMETIC

A Yale graduate, perusing the want ads in a metropolitan journal, saw one that seemed promising. "Wanted," it read, "a bright Harvard man or equivalent." When he went for an interview, he asked about the qualification, "Do you mean two Princeton men, or a Yale man working half time?"

3223　　KNOWING THE RIGHT QUESTION AND WHEN TO THROW IT

The insurance salesman had his man on the hook, ready to sign for a $50,000 life insurance policy, but suddenly the prospect put down the pen with which he was going to sign his name and said, "I think I'll wait until April before signing for this. Come back then."

The insurance salesman packed up his briefcase, stood up, started to leave, then stopped and asked the man, "Whom shall I ask for if you're not here in April?"

That did it. The man signed up for the insurance.

3224　　A CLERK'S PAYDAY RAFFLE—SOURCE FOR LIVING IT UP

A clerk in a department store, receiving a very nominal salary, suddenly began to lead a very gay life. He dressed in the height of fashion, bought an expensive car, and gave every evidence of having great wealth. The personnel manager kept an eye on him, and finally called him into his office.

"How is it, young man, that you, who are receiving a salary of only $25 a week, can spend what must certainly amount to well over $100 a week. Have you been left a fortune, or what's the answer?"

"It's very simple, sir," the clerk replied, unabashed; "There are more than 200 employees upstairs now, and every payday I raffle off my salary at $1 a ticket."

OFFICE HUMOR

3225　　LATE STENOGRAPHER AND FUMING BOSS

The new stenographer arrived late for work and her fuming boss said, "You should have been here at nine!"

"Why," she asked, "what happened?"

3226　　A FOUR-HOUR DAY—COFFEE BREAKS IN

A four-hour day would bring many changes in our lives. For example, we'd have to reschedule the coffee breaks.

3227　　SHE CAN'T TYPE BUT SHE'S BEAUTIFUL—RUBBER STAMP OF BOSS

A philosophical New Yorker, who gave up all hope of getting perfect letters from his office typist, now sends out the letters as they come from her—spelling errors, erasures, and all. He evens matters up with a rubber stamp that he had specially made. It marks in the lower left-hand corner: "She can't type—but she's beautiful."

3228   SELF-MADE MAN—USE OF IDLE TIME

A reporter asked a new sensation in the business world: "Mr. Warren, you are truly a self-made man. You have educated yourself while you fought your way up to success. Tell me, how did you get in all that reading during those busy years?"

"It was quite simple," Mr. Warren explained, "I kept a good book open upon my desk, and read it whenever someone said to me over the telephone, 'Just a moment, please.'"

3229   GETTING ALONG WITH DAD—THE PRESIDENT

After three months of work, the young fellow was called to the office of the president, who said to him, "You have been working here now for three months. Have you been getting any attention?"

The young fellow said honestly, "No, sir—not even one little promotion or increase in pay."

"Well," said the president, "I am going to make you a vice-president and increase your salary $20,000 a year."

"Gee, thanks," said the young fellow.

"Is that all you can say?" asked the president.

"Oh, no," was the reply. "Gee, thanks, Dad."

3230   HONESTY IS THE BEST POLICY

The successful businessman was arguing with a competitor and burst forth with:

"I'll tell you one thing; there are lots of ways of making money, but there is only one honest way."

"What way is that?" asked his competitor.

"Just as I suspected," snorted the first man. "You don't know!"

3231   HOW TO BE A SUCCESS

"I owe much of my success to a 220-pound bully who kicked sand in my face at the beach when I was a mere 100-pound kid."

"What did you do? Build yourself up and then lick the guy?"

"Oh, no," replied the successful man. "I determined to work hard, save my money, invest it wisely—and now I have my own private beach."

3232   GOING OVER BOSS'S HEAD

The tyrannical boss called in his chief clerk and said, "Wilkins, I understand that you have taken to praying for a raise. Now I want you to understand once and for all that I will not tolerate your going over my head."

3233   RESPONSIBLE MAN WANTED

"We wanted a responsible man for this job," said the employer to the applicant.

"Well, I guess I'm just your man," said the young fellow, "No matter where I worked, whenever anything went wrong, they told me I was responsible."

OPTIMISM AND PESSIMISM

3234   POTATO CROP ACCORDING TO SIZE

Two amateur gardeners met on the street. Asked one, "How did your potato crop turn out?"

Replied the other, always an optimist: "Splendid. Why, some are as big as marbles, some as big as peas, and, of course, quite a lot of little ones."

3235   WIFE AND CIGAR BUTTS

An optimist is a man who concludes his wife has given up cigarettes because when he got home from a trip he found cigar butts all around the house.

3236   FISH STORY

"How many fish have you caught?" asked someone seeing an old villager fishing on the banks of the stream.

"Well, sir," replied the old fisherman thoughtfully, "if I catch this one I'm after, and two more, I'll have three."

3237   MORE STARTING TIME NEEDED

A young boy ran desperately up to the train platform just in time to see the last car pull away.

A man standing on the platform smiled sympathetically and said, "What a shame, I guess you didn't run fast enough."

Replied the boy firmly, "Oh yes I did, I just didn't start soon enough."

3238   WILD MEN AND WILD WOMEN

An optimist and a pessimist were shipwrecked and in time their raft came within sight of a tropic island. The pessimist, expecting the worst, said: "I'll bet it is inhabited with a bunch of wild men."

The optimist, forever cheerful, said: "Yes, perhaps. But, cheer up, where there are wild men—there are wild women!"

3239   EVIL EYE

A pessimist is one who likes to listen to the patter of little defects.

PLACES

3240   BIRD OF PARADISE—LONG WAY FROM HOME

A New Yorker was driving through a barren wilderness in West Texas when a fancy bird skittered past the car. "What kind of fowl do you call that?" he asked. The driver answered proudly, "That's a bird of paradise."

"Hmmm," mused the New Yorker. "Kind of far from home, isn't he?"

3241   GREAT BRITAIN IN TEXAS—DRESSING THE PLACE UP

On a train during a tour of the United States an Englishman fell into conversation with a Texan, who embarked on a long recitation of the wonders of the Lone Star State. "Maybe you didn't realize it while you were going through my state," the Texan wound up, "but all of Great Britain could fit into one corner of it."

"I dare say it could," said the Englishman dryly, "and wouldn't it do wonders for the place!"

3242   TRAINS STANDING STILL—TEXAN TOURING ENGLAND

A particularly loyal Texan was touring England not long ago, and kept himself entertained by teasing the British about their "midget" country. He irritated one man who asked him for the dimensions of his wonderful state.

"Well," drawled the big Texan, "I don't right know exactly how big she is. But I do know that I can board a train, and twenty-four hours later still be in the Lone Star State!"

"Oh really?" replied the Englishman. "We have trains like that here, too."

3243   GOLDEN FENCE AROUND TEXAS

A proud young lady from Kentucky was engaged in a conversation with a Texan. Trying to justify her state she said, "In Kentucky we have Fort Knox, where enough gold is stored to build a golden fence 3 feet high completely around Texas."

Drawled the Texan, "Go ahead and build it. And if I like it—I'll buy it."

3244   CZECH STUDENT'S QUESTION

A Russian lecturer was telling Czech students in Prague about the Soviets' wonderful scientific advances. "Already," he said, "we have launched many satellites. In no time at all we will be able to go to the moon. In a matter of a few years we will be able to go Mars, and then to Venus. And later to all the planets. Isn't this a wonderful thing?"

All the students nodded.

"Are there any questions?"

A student raised his hand. "Sir," he asked, "when can we go to Vienna?"

3245   MOSCOW FATHER'S SONS—THREE IN RUSSIA, ONE IN AMERICA

Allen W. Dulles, former director of the CIA, enjoys telling about a Moscow father who was being complimented by a neighbor on his three sons:

"You must be mighty proud of them," said the neighbor, "One of them is a comrade doctor, another a comrade lawyer, and the third a comrade artist."

He replied, "Yes, they are fine people's men but the one I am really proud of is the fourth boy, who is in America."

"He's an American capitalist!"

"Yes, indeed. He's unemployed and on relief, and if it wasn't for the dollars he sends home we'd all starve."

3246   THE IRON CURTAIN CUSTOMER—HOW MUCH FOR THE WHISTLE?

An American manufacturer was showing a prospective customer from an Iron-Curtain country through his plant. When the noon whistle blew and thousands of men hurried away, the visitor was aghast. "They're all escaping!" he cried. "Can't you stop them?"

"Don't worry," the manufacturer said. "They'll come back." The visitor looked at him skeptically, but, when the starting whistle blew, the men returned and set to work. Later in the day the manufacturer broached the subject of business. "Now," he said, "about those machines you were interested in buying. . ."

The Iron-Curtain customer interrupted him. "We'll talk about that afterward," he said, "but first tell me how much you want for that whistle!"

3247   GODSPEED—TWO FOR ONE

The nuns at a small convent were happy to learn that an anonymous donor had left his modest estate to them. Each nun had been left fifty dollars in cash to give away as she saw fit.

Each sister announced how she would spend her bequest. Sister Catherine Anne decided to give her share to the first poor person she saw. As she said this, she looked out of the window and saw a man leaning against the telephone pole across the street, and he looked poor indeed.

She immediately left the convent and walked toward the man. He had obviously known better days, and the good nun felt he had been sent by heaven to receive her offering. She pressed the fifty dollars into the man's hand and, as she did so, she said, "Godspeed, my good man," and started to leave.

"What is your name?" he called after her.

Shyly she replied, "Sister Catherine Ann," and left.

The following evening, the man returned to the convent and rang the bell. "I'd like to see Sister Catherine Ann," he said.

"I'm afraid I cannot disturb her now. She's in the chapel. May I give her your message?"

"Yeah," said the visitor gleefully, "give her this hundred bucks and tell her Godspeed came in second!"

3248   PASSING THE HAT AROUND—RETURN OF EMPTY HAT

In a tight-fisted Iowa congregation, the hat was passed around one Sunday and returned absolutely empty. The pastor cast his eyes heavenward and said reverently, "I thank thee, oh Lord, that I got my hat back."

3249   FEARFUL VISITOR IN SEARCH FOR HONEST MAN IN NEW YORK

Diogenes, still searching for an honest man, came to New York City and after his visit was asked how he made out.

"Not so bad as I feared," he replied, "I still have my lamp."

3250   COST OF SUNSET—IN FLORIDA

There's no state like Florida to empty tourists' pockets. According to one source, the manager of a large Florida motel suggested to a guest that he step outside to see the beautiful sunset.

Asked the guest cautiously, "How much will it cost?"

3251   GUADALCANAL—WISE MAN'S REFUGE

In their book, *Rascals in Paradise*, James Michener and Grove Day tell about a learned gentleman in the thirties who clearly foresaw that a great war was about to engulf the world. After consultation with several top military men he decided that his only secure refuge from the world's insanity lay on some tropical isle, far from civilization.

So, in 1939, one week before Germany invaded Poland, this wise man fled to his idyllic, almost unknown South Pacific refuge. It was an island called Guadalcanal.

POINT OF VIEW

3252   IMPORTANCE OF A POSITIVE ATTITUDE

Many of life's successes and failures depend on how you choose to interpret certain events. This anecdote will serve any speaker well in showing the importance of a positive attitude:

An old captain's schooner had sunk far off the Maine coast and his friends were helping him beach it for repairs.

Remarked one, "Too bad she had to sink, Cap'n."

"She didn't sink," the old man replied tartly, "she just didn't rise with the tide."

3253   THE CAPTAIN'S LOG—NOTHING BUT THE TRUTH

The captain of a ship once entered in his log, "Mate was drunk today." When the mate became normal, he was terribly chagrined and angry; he pleaded with the captain to strike out the record; he declared that he had never been drunk before, and promised he would never drink again. But the captain said, "In this log we always write the exact truth."

The next week the mate kept the log and in it he wrote, "Captain was sober today."

3254   REWARDS FOR VALOR—REQUESTS OF TROOPS

After the Battle of Austerlitz, Napoleon Bonaparte called representatives of various nationalities among his troops before him and told them he wanted to reward their valor by granting whatever wish they might desire.

A Pole cried out, "Restore Poland!" and a Slovak called out that he wanted a farm. A German soldier asked for a brewery.

To each of them Napoleon said gravely, "Your wish shall be granted." Then he asked a Jewish soldier what he wished for, and the Jew said he'd settle for a schmaltz herring. And Napoleon ordered that it be obtained and given to the Jewish soldier immediately.

Later, his fellow soldiers twitted the Jew for his absurd request, when he could have asked for a reward of great price and consequence.

"We shall see who is the foolish one," said the Jew. "See if Poland is freed or if the one man gets his farm and the other a brewery. In the meantime, I'm enjoying my herring."

3255   INTRAVENOUS FEEDING—FRIEND AND HIS DOCTOR

A hospitalized friend was being kept on intravenous feeding, and protested loudly that he wanted something more substantial.

"But intravenous isn't so bad," said the doctor. "It's just what you need. Now is there anything else I can do to make you happier?"

"Yes," snapped the patient, "lie down and have lunch with me!"

3256   INCONSOLABLE TRAINER ON LOSS OF AN ELEPHANT

The biggest elephant in the Berlin Zoo expired of old age, and his trainer was inconsolable. Finally the zoo superintendent told him, "It's ridiculous to carry on that way about the loss of one elephant. We expect to replace him, you know."

"Easy enough for you to talk," wailed the trainer. "Just remember who has to dig the grave!"

3257   FARMER AND HIS CHILDREN

We all know the value of a good example, and what a compliment to be considered a good example in your field. But we wonder just how flattered this man was when he was offered as a good example:

Every season out in Pomona, California, they hold a county fair that is attended from far and wide. A farmer from up in the Valley attended the fair particularly because he wanted to see the grand champion bull. And he brought his whole family. When he arrived at the entrance, he found that he and his wife and the two eldest children would have to pay fifty cents each and the other seven children twenty-five cents. Being a cattle-minded man, he kicked like a steer. The manager was going by and asked what was the matter. Said the farmer: "I and the wife and the children have travelled nigh onto 200 miles to see that champion bull, but I'm danged if I can afford to pay $3.75 to get in."

"Are all the children yours?" the manager asked.

"They certainly are," said the farmer.

"Let 'em in free," the manager instructed the gatekeeper.

Then, turning to the farmer, he said, "We want that bull to see you."

3258   SHIPWRECKED SAILOR AND BUNDLE OF NEWSPAPERS

The shipwrecked sailor had spent nearly three years on a desert island, and one morning was overjoyed to see a ship in the bay and a boat putting off for the shore. As the boat grounded on the beach an officer threw the sailor a bundle of newspapers. "The captain's compliments," said the officer, "and will you please read through these and then let him know whether you still wish to be rescued?"

3259   A YOUNG SOLDIER'S PRINCIPLES

On occasion we all find ourselves in trying situations because of our attempts to adhere to our principles. But none of our plights can match that of the young soldier described by General Pershing:

General Pershing was on a tour of inspection on the Western Front. Stopping at one of the camps that housed the wounded, he happened to notice a very bedraggled looking soldier sitting outside one of the tents. The General was just about to remark sympathetically about his condition, having noticed that he had one arm in a sling and a huge bandage about his head, when he heard the man muttering to himself.

"I love my country," Pershing heard the man say, "I'd fight for my country. I'd starve and go thirsty for my country. I'd die for my country. But if ever this damn war is over, I'll never love another country again!"

3260   INSTRUCTION FROM BANDLEADER TO MUSICIANS

The divorce rate rises each year and to most of us these are depressing statistics. But we know of one man who can even see a light side to that:

A famous society bandleader whose nine orchestras have played for some 10,000 weddings over the years instructs his musicians: "Always play your best. Remember, one out of every five brides gets married again!"

3261   VARIOUS WAYS OF INSULTING SALESMEN

Asked an old-timer of the new salesman, "How are you getting along?"

Replied the new salesman with disgust: "I've been insulted in every place I made a call."

"That's strange," said the old man. "I've been on the road over 40 years. I've had my samples flung in the street, been tossed downstairs, manhandled by janitors, and rolled in the gutter, but insulted—never!"

3262   ODDEST THING ABOUT AMERICANS—PECULIAR SLANT OF EYES

A Chinese delegate to the U.N. was besieged by reporters when he arrived in N.Y. One of the questions flung at him was: "What strikes you as the oddest thing about Americans?"

He thought for a moment, then smiled. "I think," he said, "it is the peculiar slant of their eyes."

3263   GLORY OF A SNOB—DOCTOR'S DIAGNOSIS

A snob walked into a doctor's office and said, "Doctor, I feel terrible. I want you to give me a thorough examination and tell me what is wrong with me."

"Fine," said the doctor. "But first let me ask you a few questions. Do you drink much liquor?"

"I have never touched the vile stuff," the man replied indignantly.

"Do you smoke?" the doctor continued his inquiry.

"I have never touched the filthy weed!"

"Do you run around much at night?"

"Of course not! I am in bed every night by ten o'clock for a good night's rest."

"Tell me," the doctor continued, "do you have sharp pains in the head?"

"That's just it," the snob replied. "I have sharp pains in the head."

"That's your trouble, my dear man," the doctor said, "your halo is on too tight."

3264   WATCHING THE CARS AND FENCES GO BY

A motorist driving along a busy country highway one Sunday morning, stopped to ask directions from a man sitting on a fence, smoking a pipe and looking at the traffic.

"I just don't see how people stand living in the country," said the motorist. "There's nothing to see, nothing to do. Why, I'm on the go all the time."

The fellow on the fence looked disdainfully at the stranger and drawled, "Well, I don't see any difference in what I'm doing and what you're doing. I sit here on the fence and watch the cars go by. You sit in your car and watch the fences go by. It's the way you look at things."

3265   RECOVERING LOST PASSENGERS

A boatman ran a ferry across a mountain stream full of whirlpools and rapids. During a crossing in which the frail craft was tossed about by the swirling waters, a timid lady in the boat asked whether any passengers were ever lost in the river.

"Never," the boatman reassured her. "We always find them again the next day."

3266   HIGH MILEAGE OF FOREIGN CARS

I bought an English-made automobile and after careful computation over a month concluded that I was not getting the phenomenally high mileage so often credited to such cars. So I took it to a local mechanic who, after checking it thoroughly, pronounced it in perfect condition.

"I love the car," I confessed, "but isn't there *something* I can do to increase its mileage?"

"Well, yes," he said. "You can do the same as most foreign car owners do."

"What's that?" I asked.

"You can lie about it," he replied.

3267   FISH STORY

Mr. Jones and Mr. Glover were lunching together. As their various friends passed the table, Mr. Jones would stop them and, in glowing terms, describe his success on his recent fishing trip.

Glover, amused by the enthusiastic Mr. Jones, finally said, "Say, I notice that in telling about that fish you changed the size of it for each different listener."

"Yes, sure, I never tell a man more than I think he will believe."

POLITICS

3268   TWO REPUBLICAN VOTES

In a local election in Mississippi, officials tabulating the ballots were astounded to discover a Republican vote. There being no precedent for this phenomenon, the sheriff decided, "Let's hold it out till we get a full count." Then—wonder of wonders!—another Republican vote turned up. "That settles it," roared the sheriff. "The low-down varmint voted twice, so we won't count either of them."

3269   BREAKING IN—FOR DOING NOTHING

"I was in Washington recently," claims comedian Stu Allen, "and thought I might go into politics. I talked to one of the big men there, and he asked me what I could do. I said, 'Nothing' and he said 'Wonderful. Then we won't have to break you in.' "

3270   APPOINTED POLITICAL JOKES—PRESIDENT HARDING ON

When Will Hays took Will Rogers to the White House to meet President Harding, Rogers said, "Mr. President, I would like to tell you all the latest political jokes."

"You don't have to, Will," said Harding with a touch of bitterness, "I appointed them."

3271   WHO CREATED CHAOS?

A doctor, an engineer, and a politician were arguing which of their professions was the oldest.

The doctor said, "Of course, medicine was the oldest. Mankind has always had physicians, and they are even mentioned in the Bible."

"That's nothing," said the engineer. "The Bible tells how the world was created out of chaos, and how could there be any order brought out of chaos without an engineer?"

"Hey, wait a minute," said the politician. "Who do you **think** created the chaos?"

3272   SEEING LIGHT—GETTING HOT

A politician who had changed his views rather radically was congratulated by a colleague. "I'm so glad you've seen the light," he said.

"I didn't see the light," was the quick reply. "I felt the heat."

3273   DEMANDING NEWSPAPER EDITOR'S APOLOGY

Politician: "What do you mean by publicly insulting me in your old rag of a paper? I will not stand for it and I demand an immediate apology."

"Just a moment," answered the editor. "Didn't the news item appear exactly as you gave it to us, namely, that you had resigned as city treasurer?"

"It did, but where did you put it?—in the column headed 'Public Improvements.'"

3274   SENATOR RUNNING FOR RE-ELECTION—CALLING PEOPLE BY FIRST NAMES

A group of reporters waited outside the office of a senator campaigning for re-election. Suddenly the door flew open. "Quick!" the candidate shouted to his secretary. "Where's that list of people I call by their first names?"

3275   FISHING FROM TWO SIDES OF WATER—OPEN MOUTHS

At a little stream on the Swiss frontier, a Swiss and a Nazi were fishing from the opposite sides of the water. Great success had attended the Swiss, and he had a handsome string to show for his efforts; whereas the Nazi had not had so much as a nibble.

"Why is it," called the German across the water, "that you have so much better luck? Are we not using the same bait?"

"Well," said the Swiss, "on this side the fish aren't afraid to open their mouths."

3276   DODGING ISSUES—SENATORIAL CANDIDATE'S SPEECH

Admirer to senatorial candidate after speech: "Great speech, sir—I liked the straightforward way you dodged those issues."

3277   CANDIDATE AND LOG CABIN

A candidate for a high state office in Arkansas was accused by his opponent of merely posing as a "son of very poor parents." "As a matter of fact," thundered the opponent, "my adversary comes from the richest family in his country." The candidate answered calmly, "It's quite true I wasn't born in a log cabin. But we moved to one as soon as we could afford it."

3278 THE DEVIL AND HELL—MAN'S CHOICE OF SECTION

In Russia they're telling a story of a man who, arriving in hell, is asked by the devil which section he wants to go to, capitalist or communist. "The communist hell, of course," he replied, "I know the heating won't work."

3279 SAVING BOTH FACES—FAMOUS POLITICIAN

And then there was the famous politician who was trying to save both his faces.

3280 ILLINOIS LICENSE PLATES—WORDS APPEARING

The words, "Land of Lincoln" have been appearing on Illinois license plates ever since a 1955 Act of Congress granted the state a copyright to use them.

Getting the law through Congress was a snap compared to the tussle in getting it through the Illinois State Legislature. First off, the Democrats wanted to make it "Land of Lincoln and Douglas." Then a legislator who sold cars between sessions proposed "Land of Lincoln, Mercury and Ford."

3281 TODAY'S LEADER AND PEOPLE

The trouble with being a leader today is that you can't be sure whether the people are following you or chasing you.

3282 SEEKING VOTER—POLITICIANS

Politicians are noted for their fence-straddling in seeking votes. One particularly experienced politician once spoke before a convention of commercial artists. He was asked to name his favorite color. With no hesitation he replied, "Plaid."

3283 POLITICAL RALLY OR FUNERAL

When W. B. Harsfield was Mayor of Atlanta, he related that his first venture into politics was as a candidate for the City Council of Atlanta. On every crowded street corner and every public gathering, he passed out cards and campaign material, greeting everyone. One day a friend told him a political meeting was being held on a certain residential street, but the fellow was not certain of the address. When Hartsfield came upon a number of parked cars and a crowd, he swung into action dealing out cards and shaking hands. But he was stung by the cool reception he got; the more he smiled, the more frigid. Finally on the steps of the house he mumbled, "This isn't much of a political rally—it's more like a funeral."

"Brother," a nearby voice retored gruffly, "this *is* a funeral!"

3284   WHAT ARE YOU—REPUBLICAN OR DEMOCRAT?

When Franklin D. Roosevelt was running for a third term on the Democratic ticket, a Republican candidate for the Legislature in Vermont declared he was supporting F.D.R. for the presidency. A Vermont Republican challenged this man's divided party loyalty. "What are you," he asked the candidate, "a Republican or a Democrat? I want an honest answer."

"I'll give you an honest answer," said the candidate; "I am a politician."

3285   MEMBERS OF THE UNITED STATES CONGRESS—AMERICANS OR INDIANS

"I am here," said the Indian to the Congressional committee, "on behalf of my people to urge that they be given the right to manage their own lands the same as all other Americans."

Said one of the Senators: "Well, I am not convinced that the average Indian is competent enough to handle property."

Replied the Indian representative, "Do you mean to suggest, Senator, that I am not capable—that I am a man of less-than-average intelligence?"

"Oh, I was referring to the *average* Indian," said the Senator. "You are not average. You are well above average. You would not be here representing your tribe if you were not one of the smartest people in it."

"You are wrong, Senator," replied the Indian. "Indians are no different than other Americans. They never send their best minds to the United States Congress."

3286   MESSIAH AND BEN GURION—DIFFERENCE BETWEEN

An Israeli who once compaigned against Ben Gurion in an election said: "The difference between the Messiah and Ben Gurion is that the Messiah refuses to come and Ben Gurion refuses to go."

3287   PAYOFF FROM THE GOVERNMENT

Good government pays. The other kind does, too, but not the same people.

PRAYER AND RELIGION

3288   THE KEYS TO HEAVEN AND HELL

A repentent sinner once said to Father Callahan, "Reverend Father, I wish you were St. Peter."

"Why?" said the priest.

"Because, then you would have the keys to heaven to let me in."

"Actually," replied Father Callahan, "I need the keys of another place, then I could let you out."

3289   GOD OR THE DEVIL

The parish priest got a hurried call to come to the home of Chris McManus, who was dying. Chris had not exactly lived an exemplary life and his priest knew it. He looked at the dying man and said, "Chris, you've been a stormy man most of your life. Now you have only one choice, God or the devil?"

Chris slowly lifted his eyelids, looked at the priest and whispered, "Father, I'm in no position to antagonize anybody."

3290   UNIQUE WAY OF OBTAINING CONTRIBUTIONS

Said the preacher to the organist: "And when I get through with my sermon, I'll ask those of the congregation who want to contribute toward the mortgage on the church to stand up. But in the meantime, you play the appropriate music."

Asked the organist, "What do you mean, appropriate music?"

Replied the preacher, "Play the Star Spangled Banner!"

3291   FOOD AND FLOWERS ON GRAVES—CHINESE AND AMERICAN CUSTOMS

A Chinese servant asked permission of his American master to attend the funeral of a friend, also Chinese. The man gave his permission and jokingly added, "I suppose you will follow the old Chinese custom of putting food on the grave."

"Yes, sir," was the answer.

"And," still laughing, the man said, "when do you suppose the food will be eaten?"

Replied the servant, "As soon, sir, as the friend you buried last week will smell the flowers you put on his grave."

PUBLIC SPEAKING

3292   A SCHOLAR GIVING A LECTURE

At a large gathering of mathematicians, a scholar undertook to lecture on the meaning of Einstein's theories. After he had droned on for well over an hour, someone interrupted him and said, "I think you must be greater than Einstein himself. Twelve men understand Einstein—but nobody understands you."

3293   IN POSITION OF THE PARSON

Sir Joshua Stamp, in a speech at the Chicago Club, expressed a hope that he wasn't talking too long. "I wouldn't like to be in the position of the parson," he explained, "who in the midst of an interminable sermon, suddenly stopped to chide: 'You know I don't mind a bit having you look at your watches to see what time it is, but it really annoys me when you put them up to your ears to see if they are still running.'"

3294   WHAT IS A PUBLIC SPEAKER

"Public speakers should speak up so they will be heard, stand up so they can be seen, and shut up so they can be enjoyed."

3295   REVEREND SMITH—REPEATED SERMON

A minister was asked to address the graduating class in a small town about 100 miles away. He knew no one there and wondered why he had been chosen.

On graduation night, the principal began his introduction. "Reverend Smith does not know it, but about a year ago I was in his community on a Sunday morning and I dropped in at his church service. The sermon I heard was so fine I decided this was the man we wanted to speak to us at our next graduation exercise." For the next five minutes he gave a fully accurate and complete outline of the sermon of the previous year.

The waiting speaker grew paler with each flattering word. Little did anyone know that the address he had in his pocket was the sermon being so carefully outlined to the waiting audience!

3296   NERVOUS SPEAKER IN WRONG ROOM—LADIES ROOM

Upon entering a room in a Washington hotel, a woman recognized a well-known government official pacing up and down and asked what he was doing there. "I'm going to deliver a speech shortly," he said.

"Do you usually get very nervous before addressing a large audience?"

"Nervous?" he replied. "No, I never get nervous."

"In that case," demanded the lady, "what are you doing in the Ladies' Room?"

3297   JOB TO BE FINISHED—AT SAME TIME

The speaker began, "Each of us here has a job to do in this hour. Mine is to talk and your is to listen. My hope is that you will not finish your job before I finish mine."

3298   FLATTERING INTRODUCTION

Response to a flattering introduction: "I'm sorry my mother isn't here. She would have believed all the nice things the chairman said about me in his introduction."

3299   FEELINGS ABOUT INTRODUCTION

A speaker who had received an introduction that he felt promised more than he could deliver, stated his feelings thus: "I passed a small church displaying a large sign. It read: 'Annual Strawberry Festival' and below in small letters, 'On account of the depression, prunes will be served.' "

3300   LENGTH OF SPEECH—CHANGE OF

A movie executive famous for long after-dinner speeches suddenly became noted for his brevity. When asked about his reformation, he replied: "It was a remark I overheard during a pause in one of my speeches. One man said to another, 'What follows this speaker?' and the other fellow replied, 'Wednesday.' "

3301   AMERICAN MAYOR'S SPEECH—APPLAUSE

I was a member of a party of American mayors that once visited France. In Paris I was called upon to make a speech. I spoke for 15 minutes. There wasn't a bit of applause. I sat down and another man delivered a fiery oration in French. He was applauded at every pause. I joined in the applause until a neighbor whispered, "I wouldn't applaud so much if I were you, Mayor; that man is interpreting your own speech."

3302   AUDITORIUM—MEANING OF

Once when Harry Collins Spillman was introduced to a meeting in an auditorium, he began: "I am delighted to have the privilege of speaking to you today in this magnificent auditorium. I presume you know the meaning of the word *auditorium*. It is derived from two Latin words—*audio*, to hear, and *taurus*, the bull."

3303   MOTHER HUBBARD AND FRENCH BATHING SUIT

Asked at a recent gathering what sort of speech he intended to make, General Carlos Romulo, President of the United Nations General Assembly during the late 1949 session, said: "I have two types. My Mother Hubbard speech is like the garment—it covers everything and touches nothing. Then there's my French bathing suit speech—it covers only the essential parts."

3304   TOASTMASTER'S INTRODUCTION—SPEAKER'S REMARK

It was a dinner commemorating the 25th anniversary of a college organization, and the toastmaster introduced the speaker with great fervor, stressing her years of faithful service to the club and eulogizing her ability and charm. Somewhat overwhelmed, the speaker faced the audience. "After such an introduction," she said, "I can hardly wait to hear what I'm going to say."

3305   PARISHES' TIME SIGNALS—COUGHS AS

An elderly priest and a young priest were discussing the parishes. The young priest mentioned the fact that, the previous Sunday, he noticed that so many of his parishioners had colds.

"Father," said the older man, "I trust I may not sound irreverent. But as time goes on, I'm sure you'll begin to realize that not all those coughs are colds; a lot of them are time signals!"

3306   WHAT TO TALK ABOUT

The Catholic Digest mentioned a large banquet at which several long-winded speakers covered almost every subject possible.

When yet another speaker arose, he said, "It seems to me everything has already been talked about, but if someone will tell me what to talk about, I will be grateful."

From the back of the room a slightly inebriated man shouted, "Talk about a minute!"

3307   WHAT TO DO WHEN YOU ARE FULL OF BULL—MORAL

A lion sprang upon a bull and quickly devoured him. After this magnificent feast, he felt so good that he roared and roared. The noise attracted some hunters and they then killed the lion. The moral of which is that when you are full of bull, keep your mouth shut.

3308   DARROW'S SPEECH AT WOMEN'S CLUB MEETING—ON PHOENICIANS

The famous lawyer, Clarence Darrow, was once asked to address a women's club meeting. He chose to speak on the Phoenicians. His talk was vivid, his audience spellbound, and at its conclusion he was greeted with thunderous applause. The club chairman interrupted the applause to ask, "How can we express our appreciation to Mr. Darrow for such a wonderful, wonderful speech?"

Darrow rose to his feet, and announced: "Ladies, I forgot to mention a most important point in my talk. The Phoenicians invented money."

3309   JOKE, LAUGHTER, AND BROKEN GLASSES

There is a story told about New York's former Mayor John F. Hylan concerning his custom of having all his speeches written for him by a ghost writer. He had so much confidence in his ghost writers that he delivered his speeches without reading them first. However, on one occasion while reading a speech he came upon a joke he had never heard before. He began to laugh, and laughed so hard that he broke his glasses and had to have an assistant finish reading the speech!

3310   PARATROOPER GOING THROUGH HELL FOR US—NEIGHBORS TO DO THE SAME FOR HIM

Shortly after the end of World War II, a former paratrooper who had returned home was called upon to give a speech. He was scheduled for last in the evening's program, and some of the people got up to leave. The chairman of the meeting arose and announced: "I ask you people to come back and take your seats, every one of you! This good neighbor of ours went through hell for us, and it is up to us to do the same for him now."

3311   SPOKE AND TIRE—REASON FOR BRIEF SPEECH

The president of a large tire manufacturing company began his speech with the following: "I will be brief because, as is well known in our business, the longer the spoke, the bigger the tire."

3312   KISSING PART OF THE ANATOMY

Asked to introduce the chairman of a well-known club, the effusive lady had this to say:

"Oh, ladies and gentlemen, it is a great honor to introduce Mr. Howard. As you may know, in China there is an ancient custom that parents must kiss their offspring on that part of their anatomy through which they hope that the children will become famous.

"If they want their child to be a philosopher, they kiss him on the forehead. If they want him to be an orator, they kiss him on the mouth. If they hope he'll be a singer, they kiss him on the throat.

"Now I don't know what part of his anatomy Mr. Howard's parents kissed him on, but he certainly makes a wonderful chairman!"

3313   SPIRIT OF THE OCCASION

One of New York's leading clergymen was invited to address a luncheon meeting of a ladies' group at a Brooklyn church. He was asked to discuss specifically China and Chinese philosophy. He was a bit mystified since he knew so little about China, but anxious to oblige, he spent two weeks in diligent, thorough research.

Just before the luncheon he asked the chairman why he had been requested to talk on China—such a scholarly topic. "Oh," she explained, "we so wanted to preserve the spirit of the occasion. It's to be a chow mein luncheon."

3314   USE OF LEGS

A dinner was held in honor of the winning members of the track meet. It was attended by a large number of people and various honors were presented—each accompanied by a toast. At the close of the evening the prize honor of all, a beautiful silver cup, was awarded to the young man who had won the mile run—the major event of the meet.

The boy accepted the cup and a toast was proposed amid shouts of "Speech! Speech!" He stood up and said:

"Gentlemen, I have won this cup by the use of my legs. I trust I may never lose the use of my legs by the use of this cup!"

3315   WIFE SLANDERED OR SLAUGHTERED—HUSBAND'S REACTION

The speaker, an overpowering woman, shouted at her audience, "Is there a man here who would let his wife be slandered and say nothing?"

At the back of the room a little mousey man stood up.

The speaker stared coldly at the man and asked, "Do you really mean to say you would let your wife be slandered and say nothing?"

"Oh, I'm very sorry," apologized the small man. "I thought you said slaughtered."

3316   THE ENDLESS SPEECH

"Has he finished yet?" one suffering listener asked of another as he was leaving the auditorium by a side door.

"Yes," replied the other who had preceded him. "He finished long ago, but he just won't stop."

3317   THE TIRESOME SPEAKER

The following was one of Mark Twain's favorite stories, and is a delightful anecdote which belongs in the repertory of all public speakers.

Mark Twain had attended a meeting where a missionary had been invited to speak. Twain was deeply impressed. Later he related:

"The preacher's voice was beautiful. He told us about the sufferings of the natives, and he pleaded for help with such moving simplicity that I mentally doubled the fifty cents I had intended to put in the plate. He described the pitiful misery of those savages so vividly that the dollar I had in mind gradually rose to five. Then that preacher continued, and I felt that all the cash I carried on me would be insufficient, so I decided to write a large check."

"Then he went on," added Twain. "He went on and on about the dreadful state of those natives, and I abandoned the idea of a check. And he went on. And I got back to five dollars. And he went on, and I got back to four, two, one. And still he went on. And when the plate came around—I took ten cents out of it."

3318   SEEN, HEARD, AND APPRECIATED

At a dinner celebrating athletic stars, Helen Wills Moody finally got to her feet at the end of a long program and won everybody's heart by saying, "To be seen, one must stand up—to be heard, one must speak clearly—but to be appreciated, one must sit down."

3319   OPENING REMARKS TO LITTLE AUDIENCE

Orson Welles once lectured in a small midwestern town before an audience sparse almost to invisibility. He opened his remarks with a brief sketch of his career: "I'm a director of plays, a producer of plays. I'm an actor of the stage and motion pictures. I'm a writer and producer of motion pictures. I write, direct and act on the radio. I'm a magician and painter. I've published books. I play the violin and the piano." At this point he paused and surveyed his audience, saying, "Isn't it a pity there's so many of me and so few of you!"

3320   THE PARROT—POOREST FLIER AND BEST TALKER

After their success at Kitty Hawk with their first plane, the Wright brothers were wined and dined in Europe and were particularly well entertained in Paris. At one banquet there were speeches made by prominent statesmen, and this included one long address by a Frenchman who dwelt chiefly on the successes of the French in the fields of engineering and science, and the general superiority of Frenchmen. Almost nothing was said in the way of complimenting the Wright brothers, who were the guests of honor. Wilbur Wright was then called to speak, and he said the following:

"As I sat here listening to the speaker who preceded me, I heard comparisons made to the eagle, to the swallow, and to the hawk, as typifying skill and speed in the mastery of the air; but somehow or other *I* could not keep from thinking of the bird which, of all the ornithological kingdom is the poorest flier and the best talker —the parrot."

REAL ESTATE

3321   VALUE OF ROCKS

There was a very foxy realtor who was trying desperately to sell a rocky farm in the Ozarks. He explained to the innocent customer that the flint rocks in the soil were necessary to crop productivity and that without them the land was not much good. He said, convincingly, "Stones retain moisture, prevent erosion, and contribute minerals to the soil."

However, at that moment in the distance a man from the farm began to load some rocks into a wagon. "Let's get out of here," said the salesman to his prospect. "We don't want to get involved in a court trial as witnesses. That fellow over there is stealing those rocks!"

3322   COLLAPSE OF FIRST MODEL HOUSE

A large subdivider and developer was told by his superintendent that, when the first model house was sold and the scaffolding removed, the whole house had collapsed.

"How many times must I tell you," screamed the boss, "don't take the scaffolding away until the wallpaper is up!"

3323   ALL I NEED IS A GARAGE

A real estate agent once asked a woman if he could interest her in buying a home. "No!" she replied. "What do I need a home for? I was born in a hospital, educated in college, courted in an automobile, and married in a church. I live out of tin cans, cellophane bags, and delicatessen stores. I spend my mornings at the hairdresser's or at the golf course, my afternoons at the bridge table, my evenings at shows or movies. When I die, I'm going to be buried from the undertaker's. I don't need a home—all I need is a garage!"

RESTAURANTS AND WAITERS

3324   RETURN OF THE BENT STEAK

The meek little gent in the restaurant finally sighed and decided to give up his steak. It was tougher than sole leather. He called the waiter and pleaded that it be taken back to the kitchen. The waiter dolefully shook his head and said, "I'm sorry, sir, but I can't take it back now. You've bent it!"

3325   DINER FOUND HIS STEAK

Waiter: "And how did you find your steak, sir?"
Diner: "Why, I just moved this little piece of fried potato, and there it was!"

3326   RECALCULATING TAB FOR TIP

A young man visiting a New York night club was very much embarrassed when he discovered that he had miscounted the amount of money he had brought. He had just enough to pay for the large check but not enough left over for a tip.

There seemed no way out of the predicament, and he decided he'd best explain it to the waiter. He called the waiter over and apprehensively explained the fix he was in.

The waiter accepted his embarrassed apologies, and as he picked up the tab, murmured, "Don't let a thing like that bother you so much. I'll just add this darn thing up again!"

3327   NAME OF MELODY BEING PLAYED

While dining in a large restaurant a group of businessmen recognized a melody being played by the musician walking around playing soft dinner music. Although the melody sounded very familiar, no one could think of the name. Beckoning to the head waiter they asked him to find out what the man was playing. He marched across the dining room and then returned to announce, "Violin!"

3328   SPIKED DESSERT—MIXUP IN SERVING

A group of ministers and a group of salesmen were holding conventions in the same hotel. The two organizations held their banquet dinner at the same time—and the catering department had to work at top speed serving food to both.

The salesmen were having "Watermelon Delight" for dessert—which consisted of watermelon spiked with vodka. Not long after it had been served the frantic chef realized that it was being served to the ministers by mistake.

He grabbed a waiter, "Quick. If they haven't eaten the watermelon, bring it back and we'll give it to the salesmen."

The waiter returned in a minute to report that it was too late—the ministers were already finishing the spiked dessert.

"Good grief!" exclaimed the chef, "Did they say anything? Did they like it?"

Replied the waiter: "I don't really know how they liked it, but they are putting the seeds in their pockets."

3329   BREAD LOVER IN LOCAL RESTAURANT

A regular patron at a local restaurant complained one day that only one piece of bread was served with his meal. The next day the waiter brought him four slices.

"Better," said the customer, "but not enough. I like bread."

The next night the waiter brought him a dozen slices.

"This is better yet," said the man. "But why are you skimping? I love bread."

The exasperated manager then told the waiter, "We'll fix him!" He ordered a gigantic loaf of bread especially baked—six feet long and a thick as a barrel. When the man came in for a meal, the waiter lugged in the entire, uncut loaf, dropped it on the table, and waited hopefully for comment.

The man glared at the loaf and said bitterly, "Well, I see we're back to one piece again."

RETORTS

3330   FEAR OF FALLING OFF CAN

At a party one guest completely monopolized the conversation, much to the annoyance of the hostess's elderly mother. By the time he launched into a story of his experiences during the war, she was bored to the point of retaliation. "I was torpedoed in the Pacific," he began. "In fact, I lived for a week on a can of sardines."

"Really!" exclaimed the exasperated old lady. "Weren't you afraid of falling off?"

3331   KISSING ON FIRST OR LAST DATE

Overheard near the front door of a girls' college dormitory, the voices of a coed and her escort:

The girl said haughtily, "I'm sorry, but I don't kiss on the first date."

"Oh," said the boy hopefully, "Well, how about on the last one?"

3332   REJECTIONS—GEORGE HORACE LORIMER'S

The distinguished editor, the late George Horace Lorimer, was obliged, as are all editors, to reject by far the greater number of stories sent to him.

In the early days of his career when a great burden of editorial reading fell to him he once received a letter from an indignant woman, who said, "Last week you rejected my story. I know that you did not read it for, as a test, I pasted together pages 15, 16 and 17, and the manuscript came back with the pages still pasted. You are a fraud and you turn down stories without even reading them."

Mr. Lorimer replied: "Madam, at breakfast when I open an egg, I don't have to eat the whole egg to discover it is bad."

3333   REACTION TO MEANINGLESS DISCOURSE

"What this country needs is more free speech worth listening to."

3334   WHAT'S IN A NAME—SIGNATURE ON LETTER

Reverend Henry Ward Beecher entered Plymouth Church one Sunday and found several letters awaiting him. He opened one and found it contained the single word "Fool." Quietly and with becoming seriousness he announced to the congregation the fact in these words:

"I have known many an instance of a man writing a letter and forgetting to sign his name, but this is the only instance I have ever known of a man signing his name and forgetting to write the letter."

3335   ONE MOB—ONE RANGER

The following story is told about Bill MacDonald, an early Captain of the Texas Rangers. He received a request that a company of Rangers come to a nearby town to suppress a riot. He showed up himself, unaccompanied. The citizens' committee were disappointed and said, "We wanted a company, not one Ranger."

Replied MacDonald: "Well, you ain't got but one mob, have you?"

3336   ART OF BULLFIGHTING

A famous bullfighter once attended a large party in Paris, where he was cornered by a pompous lady who took him severely to task for the alleged cruelty of his art. She would not listen to his explanations, but went on and on endlessly about the "poor, helpless bulls." After a while of this, the bullfighter came to the limit of his patience.

"Madam," he said, "I cannot agree with you. I have killed many bulls, but I have always spared them the ultimate cruelty—not one did I ever bore to death!"

3337   OPERA TICKETS FOR FREE

A parishioner had sent a clergyman tickets for the opera. Finding he would be unable to use them, he phoned some friends and said:

"I have been given two tickets for the opera, but an unfortunate dinner engagement prevents me from using them. Would you like to have them?"

Replied the friend, "We would love to go, but we happen to be your unfortunate hosts."

3338   OPEN-MOUTHED AUDIENCE

A celebrated French actor once remarked after an opening night at the theatre: "Mon dieu! When I came out on the stage the audience simply sat there open-mouthed."

"Oh, nonsense!" rudely interrupted a younger rival of his, "They never yawn all at once."

3339   ANTIQUITIES AND CURIOSITIES

The quick retort is surely the mark of a brilliant wit. Oscar Wilde, known as a great wit himself, met his match while talking to a young American woman on one of his visits to the United States. He was being condescendingly nice, and at one point stated that he deplored America's lack of antiquities and curiosities.

Replied the young woman, "We shall have the antiquities in time. We are already importing the curiosities."

3340   IF I WERE ST. PETER—JAMES J. CURLEY

When James J. Curley was speaking during one of his many political campaigns in Boston, a heckler called out, "I wouldn't vote for you if you were St. Peter."

Without a moment's hesitation, Curley replied, "If I were St. Peter, you wouldn't be in my precinct."

3341   THE WINNER

There was one vacant seat near the center of our subway car. When the doors opened at the next stop, a man and a woman dashed for the seat from either end of the car. The man slid into it first, almost knocking the woman off her feet. We all watched anxiously as she turned on him. Seizing his arm, she held it high and shouted, "The winner!"

3342   KEEP MY WIFE'S NAME OUT OF THIS

When former Prime Minister Menzies of Australia was sworn into office, various representatives of the press were on hand to interview him. The reporter from the radical press said, somewhat bluntly, "I suppose, Mr. Prime Minister, that you will consult the powerful interests that control you in choosing your Cabinet?"

"Young man," snapped the Prime Minister, "keep my wife's name out of this."

3343   A NIGHT'S STAY AT THE FARMHOUSE

Daniel Webster was once bested by one of the farmers of his native state. He had been hunting at some distance from his inn, and rather than make the long trip back, he approached a farmhouse some considerable time after dark and pounded on the door. An upstairs window was raised and the farmer, with head thrust out, called, "What do you want?"

"I want to spend the night here," said Webster. "All right. Stay there," said the farmer, and down went the window.

3344 MARRIED BUGS AND FAMILIES IN LODGING HOUSE—MAXIM GORKY AS GUEST

A certain lodging house in the south of Italy had the Russian writer Maxim Gorky as its guest some years ago. He complained to the landlady "the morning after the night before" that his bed was infested by vermin. The landlady indignantly remonstrated: "No, sir, we haven't one single bug in the house."

"No, madam," Gorky agreed amiably, "they are all married and have large families too."

3345 TWO SIDES OF THE COUNTER—REMAINING ON

In one of the famous debates, Stephen Douglas charged Lincoln with having failed at everything he attempted—farming, teaching, liquor selling and the law. "It's true—every word of it," replied Lincoln. "But there's one thing that Douglas forgot. He told you I sold liquor but he didn't mention that while I have quit my side of the counter, he has remained on his."

3346 A GENTLEMAN'S WISH

There was a very prominent business executive who was known for his controlled, mild-mannered conduct. One day as he was hurrying to an important business meeting, he was involved in a traffic accident with a cab driver. The cab driver spared no profanity in telling the dignified and reserved gentleman what he thought of him and his driving. The gentleman's turn finally came and he said this: "My good man, I certainly do not condone your choice of expressions. Nor would I stoop to answer you in kind. But I will say however, it is my wish that when you arrive home tonight your mother will run out from under the porch and bite you!"

3347 TO NAME CALLING

At one point in the well known feud between the *Post* and the *Sun*, the *Post* reportedly accused the *Sun* of being a "dirty dog."

The next day the *Sun* replied in kind, pointing out to its readers the relationship between a dog and a post.

3348   SEEING IS BELIEVING

"You have no complaint," a city man said to a farmer, "you have your own milk, butter, eggs, meat and vegetables. With enough to eat and a place to sleep what more do you want?"

"Well," said the farmer, "you come around a few months from now and you'll see the fattest, sleekest, nakedest farmer you ever saw."

3349   GRAND CANYON—WONDERS OF

A staunch Republican from Maine was being shown the wonders of the Grand Canyon. "Yes, sir," said the guide. "It took about 5 million years for this awe-inspiring canyon to be carved out of the rocks."

"Hmm," added the man from Maine, "Government project, I presume."

3350   WHO SHOT YOU, TURKEY?—YOU DID, BERGEN

Bob Woodruff, the former head of Coca-Cola, invited Edgar Bergen to his plantation for hunting. Bergen, sharing a blind with one of Woodruff's friends, spotted a turkey. Both men fired, the turkey fell, and each insisted that his shot had brought it down.

"There's only one way to settle this," said Bergen. The ventriloquist stepped up to the dead turkey, propped it on his knee and asked: "Who shot you, turkey?" The turkey answered, "You did, Bergen."

3351   STRIKING UP AN ACQUAINTANCE—STRIKE ONE

A couple of men were standing around waiting at a cigar store with time on their hands, so eventually they struck up an acquaintanceship. Said the first, "Would you care to have a cigar?"

"No," replied the other, "I tried it once and didn't like it."

"Do you want a drink?" asked the first.

"No," replied the other, "I tried it once and didn't like it."

"Well," suggested the first, "would you like to play a game of billiards?"

"No, I tried the game once and I didn't like it," explained the other. "However, my son will be along soon and he may play a game of billiards with you."

The first fellow looked at his new-found acquaintance questioningly and remarked, "Your only son, no doubt."

3352   BATTLE OF WITS—UNARMED SOPHOMORE

Said the sophomore member of the debating team, "It's going to be a real battle of wits."

Replied his roommate, "How brave of you—to go unarmed."

3353 OWNER OF BIG LIMOUSINE AND OWNER OF SMALL CAR—LOUD SOUNDS

Along a country road came a $9,000 limousine. It caught up with a small car and the owner of the big limousine could not resist the temptation to slow down and tease the other driver a bit.

"Good grief, man," he said, "What is it about your car that makes such a loud rattling sound?"

Replied the driver of the small car, "That? Oh, that's the $8,000 jingling around in my pocket!"

3354 ELEPHANT IN UGLY AND TRUCULENT MOOD

A huge elephant and a tiny mouse were in the same cage at the zoo. The elephant was in a particularly ugly and truculent mood. Looking down at the mouse with disgust he trumpeted, "You're the puniest, the weakest, the most insignificant thing I've ever seen!"

Piped the little mouse in a plaintive squeak, "Well—don't forget, I've been sick."

3355 BREEDING AND OUTSIDE INTERESTS

A Chicago matron was recently seated next to a Mrs. Cabot at a Boston tea party. During the crisp exchange of conversation, Mrs. Cabot advanced the information that "in Boston, we place all of our emphasis on breeding." To which the Chicago matron responded: "In Chicago, we think it's a lot of fun, but we do manage to foster a great many outside interests."

3356 SIX INCHES TALLER—ACCORDING TO WEIGHT TABLE

We are all pretty much like the woman who stepped off the penny scales and turned to her husband. He eyed her appraisingly and asked, "Well, what is the verdict? A little overweight, eh?"

"Oh, no," said the wife, "I would not say that. But according to the weight table printed on the front, I should be six inches taller!"

3357 GUESTS TO DO THE CHORES

The late Thomas A. Edison had a very beautiful summer residence in which he took great pride. One day he was showing his guests about, pointing out all the various labor-saving devices on the premises. Turning back toward the house it was necessary to pass through a turnstile which led onto the main path. The guests soon found out that it took considerable force to get through this device.

"Mr. Edison," asked one of his guests, "how is it that with all these wonderful modern things around, you still maintain such a heavy turnstile?"

Said Mr. Edison, his eyes lighting up with laughter, "Well, you see, everyone who pushes the turnstile around, pumps eight gallons of water into the tank on my roof."

3358   REASON FOR CHANGING BABY'S NAME

"I've made up my mind what we'll call the baby," the young mother announced. "We'll call her Eulalia."

The father did not care for this choice but he was shrewd. "That's fine," he said. "The first girl I loved was named Eulalia, and it will evoke pleasant memories." The wife was silent for a moment. "We'll call her Mary after my mother," she said.

3359   THE INVENTION OF THE STORY

Expressing himself somewhat bitterly on the subject of storytellers who persistently interrupt themselves to ask if one has heard the story, Mark Twain told of an encounter with Henry Irving. The actor asked him if he had heard a certain story and Twain politely said, "No." Irving proceeded and later made the same query. Proceeding almost to the climax of his story, Irving again asked if he had heard it. Twain said, "I can lie once, I can lie twice for courtesy's sake, but I draw the line there. I can't lie the third time at any price. I not only heard the story, I invented it."

3360   REMARK FROM IRISHMAN IN GALLERY

In Boston the famous tenor Beniamino Gigli was singing "Faust." The stage of the Boston Opera House was not as adequately equipped as that of the Metropolitan. There was a trap door which sank down in order that Mephistopheles might conduct Faust to Hell. As Gigli stepped on this and began to sink, something went wrong and he became stuck midway and could not get any further, though he made every effort to squeeze through. In the midst of the predicament which was now clearly evident to all the audience, the voice of a slightly inebriated Irishman roared from the top gallery, "Thank God. I'm safe at last! Hell is full!"

3361   SHAW'S TERMS FOR HIS PLAYS—GOLDWYN'S LOVE OF ART

It is reported that Sam Goldwyn telephoned George Bernard Shaw and attempted to drive a bargain for the film rights to some of his plays. Shaw's terms were stiff and Goldwyn endeavored to whittle them down by an appeal to the artist.

"Think of the millions of people who would get a chance to see your plays who would otherwise never see them. Think of the contribution it would be to art."

"The trouble is, Mr. Goldwyn," Shaw replied, "that you think of nothing but art and I think of nothing but money."

SALESMEN

3362   THE SEVEN-IN-ONE INSURANCE AGENT

A very busy executive once took a few minutes away from his busy day to see an insurance agent. He began:

"You may well feel proud of yourself, young fellow," he said to the life insurance agent, "I've refused to see seven insurance men today."

"I know," replied the agent, "I'm them."

SECRETARIES

3363   HANDWRITING ON TELEPHONE CALL MEMORANDUM

A businessman returned from lunch and was handed a memorandum on a phone call by his secretary. "I can't read this," he complained. Replied the secretary, "Well, I couldn't understand him very well, so I didn't write very clearly."

3364   SWEET LITTLE NOTHINGS

A business executive was somewhat perturbed to notice that whenever a young shipping clerk walked by his secretary's desk, he would bend over and whisper something in her ear. And what was even more surprising was that she would whisper back.

Finally one day, his curiosity got the best of him and he went over to her desk to ask, "And what do you say when that young man whispers sweet little nothings into your ear?"

The secretary smiled and replied, "I whisper sweet little nothing-doings!"

SPEECHES

3365   BORING AUDIENCE WITH STORY

At a luncheon at the Americana Hotel for the Federation of Jewish Philanthropies, Senator Robert Kennedy was one of the speakers. Louis Nizer, who is known for his eloquence, had just completed his talk. Kennedy described his feelings about following Nizer by telling the following anecdote:

After the Johnstown flood, one of the townspeople insisted upon boring everyone with his experiences during the flood. When he died, he asked St. Peter to gather an audience so that he could tell them his story of the Johnstown flood. St. Peter agreed but warned him: "Please bear in mind...Noah will be in the audience."

3366   THE DEFEATED CANDIDATE FOR PRESIDENT AND HIS "GHOSTS" SPEECH

A recent candidate for President of the U.S. (he didn't make it) made an unexpected stop on his transcontinental campaign tour, and his "ghosts" had to whip up a speech for him. He grabbed it, stepped on to the observation platform, and began in ringing tones: "Fellow citizens! It is an unexpected thrill to greet my friends in this typical American town, so rich in history and tradition. Slip in some corny joke here..." The townspeople thought this was pretty funny; however, friendly reporters agreed not to file the story!

3367   JUDGE'S SPEECH IN TRIPLICATE—DELIVERED AND READ THREE TIMES

Ohio State University once invited a distinguished old judge to speak at a convocation. They didn't realize that the gentleman, always eccentric, had grown worse with the years, and was somewhat senile in the bargain. He seized his typescript firmly, plodded up to the lectern, and began reading in a high, cracked voice. When he got to the bottom of Page One, he turned the leaf and continued reading. It soon became apparent to the startled audience that the judge was rereading Page One. And if that wasn't enough, the third page was another duplicate! By this time, everybody realized that the typist had delivered the judge's speech in triplicate. Seventeen pages were read three times over by the unsuspecting old gentleman. The chairman then rushed out for an aspirin, and the audience rushed out to have hysterics.

3368   SERVICE LIKE WATER TO DROWNING MAN

A prominent bishop tells of the Sunday morning when he was approached after the service by an old lady, who said in a tone of appreciation, "Bishop, you'll never know what your service meant to me. It was just like water to a drowning man!"

3369   MAN RATHER GO TO HELL THAN LISTEN TO SERMON

An eloquent evangelist who was holding a meeting had been interrupted on several occasions by the departure of some one of the audience. He determined to stop it by making an example of the next person. Therefore, when a young man arose to depart in the middle of his sermon he said: "Young man, would you rather go to hell than listen to this sermon?"

The young man stopped midway up the aisle and turning slowly answered: "Well, to tell the truth, I don't know but I would."

3370   **SPEAKER IS SPEECHLESS**

"I would like to share with you a definition I just heard of 'speechless': the condition of a speaker who only wants to say a few words—over and over again for a few hours."

SPINSTERS

3371   **GETTING IN ON WORLD'S ARRANGEMENT**

Speaking to a concerned young spinster, the psychiatrist said, "In this world there's a man for every woman and a woman for every man. You can't improve on an arrangement like that."

She replied: "I don't want to improve on it. I just want to get in on it!"

3372   **NEED FOR FOUR HUNDRED ROOSTERS**

Two rather elderly spinsters, retired from teaching school, decided to buy a poultry farm. They went to a poultry farmer and explained their interest and said they wanted to buy two hundred roosters. The farmer looked surprised, laughed and then said, "Oh, two hundred hens is just fine. But you really don't need two hundred roosters!"

"We know," one of them said authoritatively, "but we know what it is to be lonely."

SPORTS

3373   **BASEBALL GREATS AND UMPIRES**

Jimmy, one of the all-time baseball greats, died and went to heaven. Before too long, he noticed that behind the pearly gates there were some excellent players. He decided to form a team. The response was enthusiastic. Just as they were about to play their first game, the phone rang. It was the devil.

"I understand that you've organized a baseball team. We have one down here that can beat yours!" advised Satan.

Unimpressed, Jimmy said, "Why, that's ridiculous. I've got all the great players that ever lived on my team!"

"Ha," bellowed the devil, "that's what you think. Don't forget, I've got all the umpires!"

3374 "PRIMITIVE SELF-EXPRESSION" OF GOLF

In the uncivilized countries, native tribes sometimes beat the ground with clubs and utter blood-curdling yells. Anthropologists call this "primitive self-expression." Over here we call it golf.

3375 "A LITTLE STIFF FROM POLO"

A noted polo player tells the following story about himself. At a certain dance, he was paired off with a woman to whom he had not been formally introduced. Somewhat apologetic, he said, "I'm afraid I am not dancing very well this evening; I'm a little stiff from polo." Whereupon his partner answered coldly, "It really doesn't make any difference to me where you come from."

3376 ADMISSION OF PROSPECTIVE TACKLE TO SCHOOL—ORAL QUESTION

A football coach accompanied a prospective tackle to the dean's office, where he attempted to get the boy admitted to school without a written examination. The boy, however, could not answer the simplest questions. In desperation, the dean asked, "How much is seven and seven?"

"Thirteen," the boy answered.

"Aw, let him in anyway, Dean," pleaded the coach, "he only missed it by two."

3377 FINDING LOST BALL—HOW ABOUT FINDING GOLF COURSE

When some golfers finally do find a lost ball, they can't find the golf course again.

3378 SWEET OLD LADY TELLING WHERE TO FIND THE GOLF BALLS

Searching frantically for almost an hour, two novices at the game of golf attempted to find their balls which they had driven into the rough.

About to give up they were approached by a sweet old lady who had been watching them sympathetically. "I don't wish to interfere, gentlemen, but would it be cheating if I were to tell you where to find the balls?"

3379 WELL, GIRLS, SHALL WE GO?—GAME WON

Coach Dana X. Bible of Texas A. and M. College delivered perhaps the quietest, shortest, most effective pep talk in recent football history. His team had been badly trounced in the first half of one of their big games. The interval between halves was one of silence and gloom in which the coach said nothing. At last, as the team prepared to go out again on the field, he looked them over slowly and deliberately and said, "Well, girls, shall we go?"

They won the game.

3380 BITING IRISH FOOTBALL CENTER—COMPLAINING YALE CENTER

Several years ago there was a particularly exciting football game between Notre Dame and Yale. The score was tied. The spectators were yelling wildly; the players were determined that their side would win.

Around the middle of the third quarter time was called at the request of the Yale center. Walking up to the referee he said, "Look here, Mr. Referee, I don't like to complain but everytime we get tangled up in a scrimmage play that big Irish center bites me. What do you think I should do about it?"

"Well," retorted the referee, "the only thing I advise is that you play him only on Fridays."

3381 OFFENSIVE OR DEFENSIVE CHAPLAIN

A sports writer for a college paper was assigned to cover the Notre Dame—Southern Methodist football game. On the train, he happened to sit next to one of the Notre Dame players.

"I understand," he said, "that you bring along a chaplain to pray for the team. I wonder if I could meet him to interview him for my paper."

"I'm sure that could be arranged," replied the pleasant young man, "but which one do you want, the offensive or the defensive chaplain?"

3382 PATIENCE FOR FISHING

Angler, "You've been watching me for over three hours. Why don't you try fishing yourself?"

Replied the onlooker, "I really haven't got the patience."

3383 HUNTER AT THE BUTCHER'S

Butcher: "I am sorry sir, but I am all out of wild ducks. But I could let you have a fine end of ham."

Customer: "No, thanks anyway. How could I go home and say I shot an end of ham?"

3384 TENNIS TECHNIQUE

A stout, bald gentleman was discussing his tennis technique. "My brain tells me:

Run forward speedily. Start right away. Slam the ball gracefully over the net."

"And then what happens?" he was asked.

"And then," the heavyset fellow replied, "my body says: Who, *me*?"

3385   HITTING THE OLD BUCK—SALT ADDED

"Well," said the old hunter, "I'm not impressed with any of the stories about people hitting game from a trifling 300 or 400 yards. Why, one day I was creeping along the trail when these old telescope eyes spots a nice buck. I rammed a charge down the gun barrel, then some wadding and a couple of ounces of salt. Then I let 'er fly—BANG—and that old buck dropped."

"That's very interesting," remarked a listener, "but why the salt?"

"Shucks, that deer was so far off I had to do something to keep the meat from spoiling before I could get there."

3386   CREATURE OF HABIT

A couple of Yogi Berra's waggish teammates on the New York Yankee ball club swear that one night the stocky catcher was horrified to see a baby topple off the roof of a cottage across the way from him. He dashed over and made a miraculous catch—but then force of habit proved too much for him. He straightened up and threw the baby to second base.

STATISTICS

3387   STATISTICS DON'T LIE

Instructor: "Now remember, men, statistics don't lie. Now, for an example, if twelve men could build a house in one day, one man could build the same house in twelve days. Do you understand what I mean? Mr. Brown, now you give the class an example."

Mr. Brown: "You mean if one boat could cross the ocean in six days, six boats could cross the ocean in one day."

3388   FAULTY CONCLUSION OF SURVEY

A commencement speaker was warning the graduates against the pitfalls of statistics. "A survey showed," he said, "that the families of Princeton graduates average 1.8 children, whereas for Smith graduates the figure was 1.4. A faulty conclusion could be drawn from these figures—that men have more children than women."

3389   OLD MEN NEVER DIE

A life insurance agent was quite surprised to see in his office an old man of 97, who wanted to take out a policy. The agent told him that, without a doubt, his application would be turned down. At this the old gentleman said with considerable annoyance, "You folks are making a big mistake. If you look over your statistics you'll find that mighty few men die after they're 97."

STUDENTS

3390   FAMILIARITY BREEDS CONTEMPT

A philosophy student at Tulane announced, "Frankly, I have nothing but contempt for both Aristotle and Plato." His professor observed amiably, "Not, I take it, the contempt which familiarity breeds...."

3391   A BAD EGG

Serious Harvard students of yesteryear strove manfully to win the approval of doughty Charles Townsend Copeland, one of the great English professors of all time. "Copey" marked up papers submitted to him so quickly that some students were convinced he read only the first few paragraphs and based his conclusions on insufficient evidence.

A senior, smarting under a scathing criticism, thought he had his tormentor dead to rights one day. "Professor Copeland," he announced in class, "I glued pages 22 and 23 of my manuscript together purposely—a fact that escaped your attention entirely. This proves you never read that far."

Copey answered calmly. "My boy, you don't have to eat a whole egg to know it's bad."

3392   COUNSEL TO NEWLY APPOINTED PROFESSOR

A mellow old college professor was asked for advice by a newly appointed one. His counsel was as follows:

"Experience has taught me more than the theoretical study of pedogogy. You will doubtless find in your teaching that when you are holding forth there will be some lad in the class who will disagree with you. You will be tempted to nail him down right then and there. Don't do it. No doubt he is the only one who is listening."

SUCCESS

3393   UP AND DOWNSTAIRS

Be nice to people on your way up because you'll meet them on your way down.

3394   BITTER WORDS OF BUSINESS MEN

Arguing heatedly, two very successful business men reached bitter words. Said one to the other, "Why, I can buy and sell you." Replied the other, "Yes, that may be. But I cannot only buy you but I could afford to keep you as well."

3395   I HAD A DREAM, PLUS BRAINS

Julius Rosenwald—the Chicago multimillionaire, who once said, "I never could understand the popular belief that because a man makes a lot of money he has a lot of brains"—was fond of telling the following story: "A certain man won a million dollars on number 14. When asked how he had figured it out, he said: " 'I had a dream. One night I saw in my dream a great big 9, and next I saw a 6, so I used my brains and figured that 9 and 6 is 14.' "

TACTFULNESS

3396   BEING FIRED FROM FIRST JOB

"One of the most tactful men I ever knew," says a California manufacturer, "was the man who fired me from my very first job. He called me in and said, 'Son, I don't know how we're ever going to get along without you, but starting Monday, we're going to try.' "

3397   COMPLIMENTING THE GIVERS OF HATS

President Lincoln, visited by two rival hatters who presented him with hats each had made, for a moment was uncertain how to compliment them. Finally he said: "Gentlemen, both hats mutually excel each other."

3398   HIGH TARIFF

"What about the tariff?" a listener asked Senator Tom Corwin. It was at that time a sensitive question, but the undaunted candidate replied: "I know some people in this audience are for a high tariff and others who are opposed to a high tariff. After considerable thought, I want everyone here to know—so am I."

TAXES

3399   REMARK ABOUT BLANK CHECK IN PAY ENVELOPE

An employee was handed a pay envelope which accidentally contained only a blank check. "Just what I thought would happen," moaned the worker. "My deductions have finally caught up with my salary."

3400   OVER 65 AND CLAIMING SEVEN CHILDREN AS DEPENDENTS

An auditor in the Manhattan district office of the Internal Revenue Service received a return from a woman over 65 claiming seven children as dependents. The auditor noted that the previous year she had claimed only two children. The woman was duly summoned and asked to explain.

"The cat had kittens," she said. The auditor replied that kittens might cost money but they can't be claimed as dependents.

"Young man, you must be mistaken," she said. "I've been claiming the parents for years."

3401   THE TAXPAYER'S WISH

The distraught taxpayer handed in his income tax return with his check to the Internal Revenue agent.

"Boy," complained the man, "the boys in Washington are a heartless bunch. They sure cleaned out my bank account!"

"Cheer up," consoled the revenue man. "Remember what Benjamin Franklin said: 'Nothing is certain but death and taxes.'"

"Yes," answered the vexed taxpayer, "I only wish to heaven they came in that order!"

**3402   PROMOTING NEW CORPORATION WITH OLD FRIENDS—
DECISION ON WHO KEEPS MONEY**

Taxes, of course, are a perpetual thorn in the side of the wealthy. A member of the class of '19 at Princeton had a hard time persuading two of his wealthiest class-mates to join him in promoting a new corporation that he hoped would earn a fortune. Both agreed the enterprise looked good, but pointed out that, because of taxes, it meant nothing more to them than additional headaches.

"I know," agreed the promoter, "but you two are my oldest friends, and I wouldn't feel right about going into this deal without you."

"All right," agreed the wealthier of the two reluctantly, "but one thing must be distinctly understood in advance if we make the money you predict—you have to keep it."

3403   GLASS OF JUICE FROM ONE LEMON RIND

A large muscular man sauntered up to a bar and said, "Give me the tallest glass you've got and a lemon." The bartender quickly did so. The huge man squeezed the lemon and got almost a pint of juice. Tossing aside the lemon rind, he said, "I'd like to see anyone else get that much juice out of one lemon!"

A little fellow, who had been quietly standing by, spoke up, "Let me have a tall glass and the lemon rind you just threw away." He then took the lemon rind and squeezed another full glass of juice from the already used rind.

Exclaimed the first man, "What! I'm astounded! I have never seen anything like that. How did you ever do it?"

Replied the small man quietly, "Well, you see, I'm with the Internal Revenue Service."

TEACHERS

3404   USE OF POWER OF OBSERVATION

A Glasgow teacher, in order to emphasize the value of observation, prepared a little cupful of kerosene, mustard and castor oil and, calling the attention of his class to it, dipped a finger into the atrocious compound and then sucked his finger. He next passed the mixture around to the students, who did the same with dire results. When the cup returned and he observed the faces of his students, he remarked, "Gentlemen, I am afraid you did not use your powers of observation. The finger that I put into the cup was not the same one that I stuck into my mouth."

3405   GRADING PAPERS

The arithmetic teacher felt like a heel when he had to mark this answer wrong:

The problem was as follows: If someone buys an article for $20.37, and later sells it for $2.97, does he make money or lose it?

The pupil certainly showed that he had given a lot of thought to the problem when he wrote on his paper: "He makes on the cents, but loses on the dollars."

3406   MESSAGE WRITTEN ON EXAMINATION PAPER

The well-loved Yale Professor, William Lyon Phelps, found this message written on a pre-Christmas examination paper:
"God only knows the answer to this question. Merry Christmas."
Dr. Phelps returned the paper to the student with this cheery notation: "God gets an A; you get an F. Happy New Year."

TRANSPORTATION

3407   WHY DON'T YOU GET OUT AND WALK?

A commuter complained to a conductor of the railroad line's terrible service. Retorted the conducter, "So if you don't like it, why don't you get out and walk?"
"I would," said the commuter. "But I'm not being picked up at the station until the train arrives."

3408   MAKING GREAT TIME BUT LOST

A man who was wildly enthusiastic about his driving ability was taking a trip with his wife. They had traveled a great distance when she consulted her map and announced that they were lost.
"What's the difference?" he said. "We're making great time."

3409   TRAIN ARRIVAL ANNOUNCED BY CONDUCTOR'S DOG

Train service in some Southern towns is less than perfect. Not long ago, a traveler was waiting for a train in a particularly small town. Three hours passed and still no train appeared. He was about to negotiate for a horse to continue his travels when the station agent advised him not to trouble, the train would be along very soon.
Asked the traveler, "How can you tell?"
"Oh, I'm pretty certain of it," replied the station agent. He pointed down the tracks: "You see, here comes the conductor's dog now."

3410   FERRY PULLING INTO SLIP

A harried commuter dashed on to the ferry slip and leaped over the water to the deck of the boat.

"Just made it!" he gasped.

"Why didn't you wait," asked a deckhand. "We were just pulling into the slip."

VOTING

3411   SECRET BALLOT IN RUSSIA

Kenneth Keating enjoys telling about a man in a small Russian village who went to the polls on election day to vote. He was handed a sealed envelope and shown where to drop it. However, instead, the peasant started to tear open the envelope.

"What do you think you are doing?" the Soviet official shouted. The peasant replied that he just wanted to know for whom he was voting.

"Are you crazy?" demanded the official. "Don't you know this is a secret *ballot*?"

3412   REASON FOR NEVER VOTING

A public-opinion-poll investigator was surprised to hear the following reply to his questions: "I never vote! It's quite a relief not to feel responsible for what goes on in Washington."

WEALTH

3413   MAKING AN IMPRESSION

A newly rich woman was trying to make an impression: "I clean my diamonds with ammonia, my rubies with wine, my emeralds with brandy, and my sapphires with fresh milk."

Replied the quiet woman sitting next to her: "I don't clean mine. When mine get dirty, I just throw them away."

3414   SENSATIONAL HOLIDAY WEEK FOR OFFSPRING

A very rich, very exclusive couple at a New Year's Eve whoop-de-do were regaling friends with details of the sensational holiday week they had provided for their offspring: the giant Christmas tree laden with trinkets; the fabulous presents; the round of theaters and parties; the special thirty-piece orchestra engaged to play for the last night of vacation.

Suddenly the wife gave an unearthly shriek. "Wilbur! Wilbur!" she cried, "I just remembered. Our children never came home from prep school!"

3415   LOCAL CITIZEN AND WEALTHY OLD BUDDY

Some people are very hard to impress, such as the local citizen whose old buddy came to town and called on him. This old buddy had made a fabulous fortune and his friend was determined not to be impressed by his wealth.

"I've got a limousine now with a chauffeur," said the returning friend.

"So what? Quite a few people got limousines with chauffeurs."

"Then you should see my house. It's got fifty rooms in it."

"Oh? I've heard of fifty-room houses before."

"I got an eighteen-hole golf course at my house."

"I've heard of houses with eighteen-hole golf courses, too."

"*Inside* the house?"

3416   CARD WITH DEAD HUSBAND

When a widow came into the Akron Social Security office to apply for benefits from her husband's account, she was asked for his Social Security card. "Oh, we were always told he should keep it with him at all times," said the widow, "and we buried it with him."

WOMEN

3417   FRAMED PICTURE OF LIGHTLY CLAD NIGHT CLUB DANCER

Frank Gilchrist, top executive of a Southwestern oil combine, has a framed picture in his office that depicts a lightly clad night club dancer showing a snapshot to her sidekick. "This is my new fiancé," she is boasting. "He's a clumsy, funny-looking lout, I'll admit. That thing behind his house in the background is an oil well."

3418   MISSING PAYMENTS

Young wife to husband: "If we miss two payments on the washing machine and one on the refrigerator, we'll have a down-payment on a TV set."

3419   TELEPHONE CALL TO GARDENER

A Dallas gardening expert got a call from a woman who asked anxiously, "Do you have to plant two seeds together to get a flower?"

3420   HUSBAND'S REPLY TO CONSULTANT

An income-tax consultant, uncertain as to whether a client's wife was entitled to double exemption for being 65 or over, wrote the husband asking for information. After some delay, he received this answer: "My wife says she is not 65 and never will be."

3421   SPLIT STOCK

An account executive of a Cincinnati stock-and-bond firm telephoned a woman client who had purchased her first stock, ten shares of Procter & Gamble, and excitedly told her that Procter & Gamble just announced they were going to split.

"Oh, what a shame!" replied the woman. "They've been together so long!"

3422   OLIVE WITH GIN AND VERMOUTH

A woman who was buying olives in a supermarket was overheard remarking to a friend: "I never liked these things until someone showed me how to fix them with gin and vermouth."

3423   PAJAMAS FOR A BACHELOR

A sweet little old lady spent days working on a pair of men's pajamas which she contributed to the Red Cross.

"I made them myself," she announced proudly.

They were perfect in every detail except that there was no opening in the front of the pants. The inspector hated to hurt her feelings, but he explained the error to her.

The dear old soul's face fell. However, suddenly she brightened. "Couldn't you give them to a bachelor?" she asked.

3424   GRADUATES' FUTURE CAREERS

A couple of sweet girl graduates were discussing their future careers. "It's me for the life of an airline hostess," caroled one. "That's the way to meet a well-heeled man-of-the-world."

"There must be a less wearing way of meeting men," pondered the other.

"Could be," said the first, "but you won't meet them strapped in!"

3425   PARKING BY EAR

When a friend drove me to town one day in her handsome new car, we were lucky enough to find an ample parking place right where we wanted to shop. My friend gaily backed in until she hit the car in back of her with a loud bang. Then she pulled forward and smacked into the car ahead. The crash drew the attention of the policeman at the corner. Noticing that he was watching us, my friend leaned out of the window and called cheerfully, "Did I park all right, officer?"

"Yes, lady," he answered, "But do you always park by ear?"

3426   KEEPING PACE WITH THE OFFICER

Then there is the woman driver who said to the cop arresting her: "But officer, I couldn't slow down while you were going so fast right in back of me!"

3427   FAITHFUL FATHER OF HIS SON—GROUNDS FOR DIVORCE

A lawyer in Las Vegas was sitting in his office one day when a beautiful woman entered and promptly announced she wanted a divorce.
"On what grounds?" asked the attorney.
She replied that she didn't think her husband was faithful.
Said the lawyer, "And what makes you think he isn't faithful?"
"Well," she replied. "I don't think he's father of his son."

3428   MAN—ACTING LIKE A LADY

A dignified and reserved gentleman decided to take advantage of a special sale on fur coats and surprise his wife with one as a present. After waiting about an hour on the fringe of a screaming, pushing mob of woman, he plunged toward the rack with both arms flying. Suddenly a shrill voice shrieked out, "Can't you act like a gentleman?"

Replied the man still plowing through the crowd, "I've been acting like a gentleman for over an hour and it got me nowhere. Now I'm going to act like a lady!"

3429   WOMEN RULING THE WORLD

A reporter asked Winston Churchill: "Do you agree with the prediction that women will be ruling the world by the year 2000?"
"Yes," said Churchill, "they will still be at it."

3430   I'M STILL ALIVE

"Mrs. Jones," asked the census taker, "I wonder if there is a mistake here. It says you have a child two years old and another four years old and yet your husband has been dead five years?"

"No, that is correct. However—I'm still alive."

3431 BIRD-BRAINED BRIDE MEETING HUSBAND'S BOSS

Mr. Smith was looking for a new job. He lost his old one when he thoughtlessly introduced his bird-brained bride to the head of the firm at an office get-together. "So you're my Henry's boss," gushed Mrs. Smith. "He's told me so much about you, Mr. Legree!"

3432 WHEN BABY WAS BORN—BAD TIME FOR FATHER

A young father was telling a group of friends what a bad time he had when his baby was born. Finally a young matron inquired: "Who had that baby, anyway?"

The young man nodded toward his wife. "She did," he answered quite seriously. "But *she* had an anesthetic."

3433 MAN SUING FOR DIVORCE—SEPARATED FIVE TIMES

In Atlanta, a man suing for divorce charged that his wife shot at him. The judge, to clear up a ~~technicality,~~ *point* asked the man when the separation from his wife began.

"She fired at me five times, your Honor," the man replied. "I started separating on the first shot. By the fifth shot, I had completely separated."

3434 HINTS ON WRITING—GOOD INTRODUCTION

The journalism professor was passing out a few hints on writing. "A good introduction," he explained, "is highly important. Always remember the young man who, desiring to marry Angus MacPherson's comely daughter, opened his interview with, "Sir, I'd like to show you how I can save you some money.""

3435 GETTING SOMEWHERE

Woman, shopping for wallpaper, to clerk, "Now we're getting somewhere—that's the exact opposite of what I want."

3436 HUSBAND'S CHRISTMAS PRESENT TO WIFE

From under the Christmas tree, a wife called in to her husband, "Here's your most beautiful present. It took me weeks to find it."

"I'll be right in to look at it," said the husband.

"Wait a minute," cautioned the wife, "and I'll put it on."

3437   ADAM AND EVE

One night Adam came home very, very late indeed and found Eve in a temper under the Tree of Knowledge. "Late again," she pouted. "I'll bet you're carrying on with some dizzy blond."

"Your accusation," countered Adam with dignity, "is not only outrageous but absurd. You know perfectly well there is nobody in this wide, wide world but you and me."

With this, Adam retired for the night. Something caused him to awaken with a start, however. There, hovering over him, was Eve—painstakingly counting his ribs.

3438   TIMID WIFE AND BILLBOARD

Timid wife (to husband who has fallen asleep at the wheel), "I don't mean to dictate to you, George, but isn't that billboard coming at us awfully fast?"

3439   BEAUTIFUL SILK CREATION—FROM POOR, LITTLE, INSIGNIFICANT WORM

A young girl was home from college for the Christmas holidays and the old folks were having a reception in her honor. During the event, she brought out some of her new gowns to show to the guests. Picking up a beautiful silk creation, she held it up before the admiring crowd.

"Isn't it perfectly gorgeous!" she exclaimed. "Just think—it came from a poor little insignificant worm!"

Her hard-working father looked a moment, then he said, "Yes—and I'm that worm."

3440   LET'S EAT OUT

Woman to bridge club members, "I have the most marvelous recipe for goulash—all I have to do is mention it to my husband and he says, 'Let's eat out!'"

3441   STALLED CAR—GAS TANK EMPTY

A garage mechanic quickly answered the emergency call from a woman motorist whose car had stalled. He responded to the call and made an examination. "Your car is out of gas," he told her.

"Will it hurt the car," she asked, "if I drive it home with the gas tank empty?"

3442   WHO WON BOUT?—RESULTS BY WIFE

A basketball coach who is also an ardent boxing fan often has to miss the fights shown on TV because of scheduled games. One night recently an important bout was coming up and he asked his wife to watch for him and tell him the results. After the game he rushed home eagerly. "Who won?" he asked.

"Oh," said his wife, "nobody won. One of the men got hurt in the first round and they had to quit."

3443   WOMAN SMOKING CIGARS

Traveling on an airplane, a man was surprised to see his seat mate who was an attractive blonde light up a fresh cigar. Unaccustomed to seeing women smoke cigars he asked her, "How did you ever begin smoking cigars?"

"Oh, it was really quite simple," she replied. "One evening my husband came home and found a lighted cigar in our living room ashtray."

3444   APPROXIMATIONS ON TREASURER'S REPORT

Matronly women's club treasurer addressing fellow members: "Before I give my treasurer's report, I want to make it perfectly clear that the exact figures I use are only approximations."

3445   WIFE AS BACK SEAT DRIVER

The role wives play in our lives should never be underestimated. For example, not long ago a motorist smashed his car by running into a telephone pole. A policeman rushed to the scene; fortunately, no one was injured.

The dazed driver was still sitting behind the wheel when the policeman drove up. The officer asked, "How did the accident happen?"

The driver did not reply for a moment. Then he pointed to the back seat and explained simply, "My wife fell asleep."

3446   PERSUADING HUSBAND TO BUY NEW CAR

The wife was trying to get her husband to purchase a new automobile, but he did not like the idea.

"Are you kidding," he exclaimed: "Buy a new car? Do you think automobiles grow on trees?"

Replied his wife, "Of course not, silly. Everybody knows they come from plants."

3447   OH BOY, IS THIS GOOD!

Two women were overheard talking on a bus. One exclaimed: "You know, I wouldn't say anything about her unless it was good, and oh boy, is this good!"

ABILITY

4401   WITH LANGUAGES

The ability to speak several languages is an asset, but the ability to keep your mouth shut in one language is priceless.

ACQUAINTANCE

4002   TO BORROW OR LEND?

An acquaintance is a person we know well enough to borrow from, but not well enough to lend to.

AD LIBBING

4003   WHAT IS AN AD-LIBBER?

"You know what an ad-libber is, folks. That's a man who stays up all night memorizing spontaneous jokes."

ADMIRATION

4004   **OF PEOPLE LIKE OURSELVES**

Admiration is the over-polite recognition of another man's resemblance to ourselves.
Ambrose Bierce

ADOLESCENCE

4005   **WHEN AS DUMB AS FATHER?**

Adolescence is the period when a boy refuses to believe that some day he'll be as dumb as his father.

ADVERSITY

4006   **ADVERSITY VERSUS PROSPERITY**

I'll say this for adversity: people seem to be able to stand it, and that's more than I can say for prosperity.
Frank McKinney Hubbard

4007   **NO WAY TO LOOK BUT UP**

When we are flat on our backs, there is no way to look but up.
Roger W. Babson

ADVICE

4008   **TO PUBLIC SPEAKERS**

Be brief, be sincere, be seated!

AFTER-DINNER SPEECH

4009   AT THE SIGHT OF BREAD CRUMBS

He loves after-dinner speaking so much, he starts a speech at the mere sight of bread crumbs.
Fred Allen

4010   ONLY A FEW WORDS TO SAY

After-dinner speaker is a person who has only a few words to say, but seldom stops when he has said them.

AGE

4011   MIDDLE AGE

Middle age is the time when a man is always thinking that in a week or two he will feel as good as ever.
Don Marquis

4012   OLD AGE

To me, old age is always fifteen years older than I am.   *Bernard Baruch*

4013   A SIGN OF AGE

A sign of old age is when you feel your corns more than your oats.

AMBITION

4014   WATCHING THE WORLD GO BY

You can stand still and watch the world go by—and it certainly will.

AMERICA

4015   A LIFETIME OF ASPIRIN

America is the conutry where you buy a lifetime of aspirin for one dollar and use it up in two weeks.   *John Barrymore*

4016   NO PARKING SPACE

The Russians will never invade us. There's no place to park.

APPEARANCES

4017   NEVER JUDGE BY

The girl who looks like a dumb blonde may really be a smart brunette.

ARGUMENT

4018   GETTING THE LAST WORD

The way to get the last word in an argument is to say, "I agree."

AUDIENCE

4019   OF ONE

The man who likes to hear himself talk always has an appreciative audience of one.

AUTOMOBILES

4020 **DYING WITH BOOTS ON**

Men still die with their boots on, but usually one boot is on the accelerator.

BACHELORS

4021 **MARRIED MAN'S QUESTION ABOUT**

The question that bothers every married man is: Why aren't all bachelors rich?

BARGAIN

4022 **DRIVING A BARGAIN**

One never knows how hard it is to drive a bargain until one buys a used car.

BASEBALL

4023 **WHERE A SACRIFICE IS APPRECIATED**

Baseball is the only place in life where a sacrifice is really appreciated.

BILLBOARDS

4024   VERSUS TREES

> I think that I shall never see
> A billboard lovely as a tree.
> Perhaps, unless the billboards fall,
> I'll never see a tree at all.
>
> *Ogden Nash*

BIRTHDAY

4025   A TOAST

> Another candle in the cake?
>   Well, that's no cause to pout,
> Be glad that you have strength enough
>   To blow the darn thing out.

BORES

4026   WHEN TO STOP

> If you haven't struck oil in your first three minutes, stop boring!
>
> *George Jessel*

4027   DESCRIPTION OF

> A bore is a person who talks when you wish to listen.   *Ambrose Bierce*

4028   DON'T TALK ABOUT OTHERS

> One thing you can usually say about bores is that they don't talk about other people.

CALIFORNIA

4043   ON LIVING IN

California is a fine place to live in—if you happen to be an orange.

Fred Allen

CARS

4044   TYPE OF CAR NEEDED

What this country needs is a car that can go no faster than its driver can think.

4045   DOING AWAY WITH PEOPLE

Cars formerly did away with horses, now they are doing away with people.

CELEBRATIONS

4046   A TOAST

Let us have wine and women,
  Mirth and laughter.
Sermons and soda water the day after.

Byron

4047   ANOTHER TOAST

Here's hoping that Hell will be as pleasant as the road that leads to it!

CHILDHOOD

4048   THAT WONDERFUL TIME

Childhood is that wonderful time when all you need to do to lose weight is bathe!

COMEDIAN

4049   HIS AMBITION

A comedian's ambition is to be healthy, wealthy and wisecracking.

COMFORTS

4050   OF A MAN AND A WOMAN

A good cigar is as great a comfort to a man as a good cry is to a woman.

Baron Lytton

COMMITTEES

4051   MOSES AND THE ISRAELITES

If Moses had been a committee, the Israelites would still be in Egypt.

J. B. Hughes

4052   HOW ONE WORKS

A committee is a gathering of important people who, singly, can do nothing, but together, can decide that nothing can be done.   *Fred Allen*

4053   DIVISION OF DUTIES

A committee of five consists of one man who does the work, three others who pat him on the back, and one who brings in the minority report.

4054   THE IDEAL COMMITTEE

To get something done, a committee should consist of no more than three men, two of whom are absent.

COMMUNISM

4055   PRIVILEGES OF VOTING

Communism is a form of government under which every citizen at election time enjoys the privilege of voting "yes."

COMMUTER

4056   RIDING TO AND FROM HIS WIFE

A commuter is someone who spends his life riding to and from his wife.
                                                                    E. B. White

COMPROMISE

4057   THE ART OF

A compromise is the art of dividing a cake in such a way that each one thinks he is getting the biggest piece.

CONFIDENCE

4058 **THAT COCKY FEELING**

Confidence is the cocky feeling you have just before you know better.

COUGH

4059 **YOU CAN'T HELP IT, BUT . . .**

A cough is something you yourself can't help, but everybody else does on purpose to torment you.   *Ogden Nash*

COWARD

4060 **THINKS WITH HIS LEGS**

A coward is one who, in a perilous emergency, thinks with his legs.

Ambrose Bierce

CREDIT

4061 **CREDIT AND CHASTITY**

Credit is like chastity: both of them can stand temptation better than they can suspicion.   *John Billings*

4062 BUYING ON TIME

The only thing some people do on time is—buy.

CYNICS

4063 LOOK BOTH WAYS

A cynic is a man who looks both ways before crossing a one-way street.

DAYDREAMS

4064 COST OF

Castles in the air cost a vast deal to keep up.   *Baron Lytton*

DEFEAT

4065 BITTERSWEET

Defeat isn't bitter if you don't swallow it.

DIETING

4066 A REDUCING EXERCISE

A good reducing exercise consists in placing both hands against the table edge and pushing back.

4067   WHAT THE COUNTRY NEEDS

What the country needs is a chocolate bonbon with a lettuce center for women on a diet.

DISCIPLINE

4068   OLD-FASHIONED STYLE

The old-fashioned parent believes that stern discipline means just what it says.

DRINKING

4069   RESPECT FOR AGE

Most people no respect for age unless it is bottled.

4070   DRINKING A TOAST

Here's to the heart that fills as the bottle empties!

4071   AND ANOTHER TOAST

Here's to a guy who is never blue,
Here's to a friend who is ever true,
Here's to a pal, no matter what the load,
Who never declines just one for the road!

EARLY BIRD

4072   REWARD?

Sometimes all the early bird gets is—up.

EDITOR

4073   THE WHEAT AND THE CHAFF

An editor is a person employed on a newspaper, whose business it is to separate the wheat from the chaff, and to see that the chaff is printed.   *Albert Hubbard*

EDUCATION

4074   LOOKING FOR POSITIONS

It's June, when 2,000,000 graduates leave college to look for positions and wind up getting jobs.

4075   HOW TO LEARN

The only way to learn anything thoroughly is by starting at the bottom, except when learning how to swim.

4076   A LITTLE LEARNING

A little learning is a dangerous thing, but at college it is the usual thing.

4077   WHILE YOU WAIT

College is just a place to keep warm between high school and early marriage.
George Gobel

EFFORT

4078   WANTING AND TRYING

People who want by the yard but try by the inch should be kicked by the foot.
W. Willard Wirtz

4079   FUTILITY

If all the people in the world would agree to sympathize with a certain man at a certain hour, they could not cure his headache.   *Edgar W. Howe*

4080   HELPLESSNESS

No one can feel as helpless as the owner of a sick goldfish.

Frank McKinney Hubbard

EGOTIST

4081   WHAT IS HE?

An egotist is a person of low taste, more interested in himself than in me.

Ambrose Bierce

ENEMIES

4082   PERSONAL MOTIVES

Never ascribe to an opponent motives meaner than your own.

James Mathew Barrie

EVOLUTION

4083   MAN'S DESCENDENTS

Ages and ages hence, no doubt it will give pain to those of orthodox belief when the assertion is made that the creatures of that period descended from Man.

EXAGGERATION

4084   REPORT OF THE FLOOD

Except for the Flood, nothing was ever as bad as reported.   *Edgar W. Howe*

EXPERIENCE

4085   RECOGNIZING MISTAKES

Experience is a marvelous thing. It enables you to recognize a mistake whenever you make it again.

4086   OBTAINING EXPERIENCE

What you get when you're expecting something else.

4087   STANDING UP FOR ONE'S RIGHTS

By the time a man learns to stand up for his rights, his arches have caved in.

4088   EXPERIENCE AS TEACHER

Experience is a hard teacher. She gives the test first and the lesson afterward.

EXPERT

4089   KNOWS MORE ABOUT LESS

An expert is one who knows more and more about less and less.
                                                          Nicholas M. Butler

FAILURE

4090   STARTED AT THE BOTTOM

He isn't a failure. He just started at the bottom and liked it there.

4091   IGNORED EXPERIENCE

A failure is a man who has blundered but is not able to cash in on the experience.   *Elbert Hubbard*

FANATIC

4092   ENERGIES AND AIMS OF

One who redoubles his energies after he has forgotten his aim.   *Santayana*

4093   WRONG AND LOUD

One who is mistaken, at the top of his voice.   *Ambrose Bierce*

FASHIONS

4094   WOMEN'S DRESSES

All women's dresses are merely compromises between the admitted desire to dress and the unadmitted desire to undress.   *Lin Yutang*

FATHERHOOD

4095   HEREDITARY GENIUS

No man says genius is hereditary until he has a son.

FISHING

4096   A TOAST

Here's to our fisherman brave,
Here's to the fish he caught,
Here's to the ones that got away,
And here's to the ones he bought!

FOOLS

4097   HOW TO CONVINCE

The best way to convince a fool that he is wrong is to let him have his way.
Josh Billings

4098   HARDEST THING TO BELIEVE

The hardest thing to believe about the Bible is that there were only two jack-asses in the Ark.

4099   A TOAST

Let us toast the fools; but for them the rest of us could not succeed.
Mark Twain

FREEDOM

4100   FOR ONESELF

Every tyrant who has lived has believed in freedom—for himself.

Elbert Hubbard

FRIENDSHIP

4101   A TOAST

Here's to you—as good as you are,
And here's to me—as bad as I am,
And as bad as I am, and as good as you are,
I'm as good as you are— as bad as I am!

4102   ANOTHER TOAST

Here's a toast for you and me:
May we never disagree;
But, if we do, then to heck with you—
So here's a toast to me!

4103   AND ANOTHER TOAST

Here's to the man who is wisest and best,
Here's to the man who with judgment is blessed,
Here's to the man who's as smart as can be—
I mean the man who agrees with me!

FUTURE

4104   TOADS AND TOADSTOOLS

Don't lay any plans for the future; it is like planting toads and expecting to raise toadstools.

Josh Billings

4105   INTEREST IN THE FUTURE

My interest is in the future because I am going to spend the rest of my life there.
                                                                          Charles Franklin Kettering

GARDENING

4106   DIFFERENCE BETWEEN WEEDS AND PLANTS

People say that they often find it hard to tell the difference between weeds and young plants. The sure way, of course, is to pull them all out. If they come up again, they're weeds.

GIVING

4107   TAX DEDUCTIBLE

Not only is it more blessed to give than to receive—it is also deductible.

4108   HELPING THE TROUBLED MAN

If you help a man who is in trouble, he'll never forgive you—especially the next time he gets into trouble.

4109   THE PHILANTHROPIST

A philanthropist is one who gives away what he should give back.

4110   MOST BENEVOLENT

He was so benevolent, so merciful a man, that he would have held an umbrella over a duck.
                                                                          Douglas Jerrold

GOLF

4111   TOOLS ILL-ADAPTED

A game in which one endeavors to control a ball with implements ill-adapted for the purpose.
Woodrow Wilson

GOOD FORTUNE

4112   A TOAST

May bad fortune follow you all your days
And never catch up to you.

GOVERNMENT

4113   SPECIFICATIONS

An elephant is a mouse built to government specifications.
Congressman William B. Widnall

4114   LOST SHEEP

If Little Bo-Peep lost her sheep today, the government would pay her for not finding them.

4115   MOVING PROJECT

A sea monster is discovered in a Scottish lake each year. It can't be a government project because it moves.

4116   THE FAMILY OF NATIONS

Someone asks, "Why can't the nations of the world live as one big family?" The answer is, "They do."

GROWING UP

4117 **WHEN A BOY BECOMES A MAN**

A boy becomes a man when he stops asking his father for money and requests a loan.

HAPPINESS

4118 **A TOAST**

A toast to five secrets of happiness: money, money, money, money, money!

HEALTH

4119 **SLEEP**

You need to start worrying about your health if you can't sleep when it's time to get up.

4120 **A TOAST**

Here's to your health! You make age curious, time furious, and all of us envious!

HUMOR

4121 **PUNS**

A pun is the lowest form of humor—when you don't think of it first.

Oscar Levant

4122   IMPROVING A JOKE

Nothing improves a joke more than telling it to your employees.

HUSBANDS

4123   LUCKY WIFE

When a husband sees the kind of men most women get, he can't help thinking his wife was lucky.

4124   WIFE'S TROUBLES

A husband is one who stands by you in troubles you wouldn't have had if you hadn't married him.

INEXPERIENCE

4125   CAREERS ENTRUSTED TO AMATEURS

The two most difficult careers are entrusted to amateurs—citizenship and parenthood.

INTELLECT

4126   KNOWLEDGE

To the small part of ignorance that we arrange and classify, we give the name knowledge.

4127   SMART OR IGNORANT?

It takes a lot of things to prove you are smart, but only one thing to prove you are ignorant.

4128   LIMITATIONS OF STUPIDITY

Genius may have its limitations, but stupidity is not thus handicapped.

4129   THINKING ALIKE

When all think alike, no one thinks very much.   *Walter Lippman*

4130   GENIUSES

With the stones we cast at them, geniuses build new roads for us.
                                                                   Paul Eldridge

4131   WORKING ON IDEAS

Ideas are funny little things that won't work unless you do.

4132   THE BRAIN

No brain is stronger than its weakest think.   *Tom Masson*

4233   SMALL HEAD, BIG DREAMS

The smaller the head, the bigger the dream.

4134   SUPERIORITY OF MEN?

The superiority of men over animals is not so clear when you consider that a cow is now milked with a machine without a man, but never without a cow.

JOURNALISM

4135   THE BIG LIE

Journalists say a thing that they know isn't true, in the hope that if they keep on saying it long enough it will be true.   *Arnold Bennett*

LAWYERS

4136   LEAVING FORTUNES

I've had ample contact with lawyers, and I'm convinced that the only fortune they ever leave is their own.

LEARNING

4137   QUESTIONS AND ANSWERS

Just about the time you finally learn the answers, they change all the questions.

LOVE

4238   COMPARED TO WAR

Love is like war, easy to begin, but very hard to stop.   *H. K. Mencken*

4139   TRIUMPH OF IMAGINATION

Love is the triumph of imagination over intelligence.   *H. L. Mencken*

4140   A DOG'S LOVE

A dog is the only thing on this earth that loves you more than he loves himself.
Josh Billings

4141   LOVE THY NEIGHBORS

The Bible tells us to love our neighbors, and also to love our enemies; probably because they are generally the same people.   *Gilbert Keith Chesterton*

4142   FEW HAVE SEEN IT

True love is like a ghost: Everybody talks about it but few have seen it.

Francois de La Rochefoucauld

4143   POWER OF LOVE

Love has the power of making you believe what you would normally treat with the deepest suspicion.

4144   APPRECIATION OF LOVERS AND LEAVERS

Some girls appreciate the man who loves them and leaves them, provided he leaves them enough.

4145   KNOWLEDGE OF LOVE

A man's knowledge of love depends on the way he grasps the subject.

MAN AND LIFE

4146   UNDERSTANDING AND LIVING

Life can only be understood backwards, but it must be lived forwards.

S. Kierkegaard

4147   FORGIVENESS OF SINS

God may forgive your sins, but your nervous system won't.

Alfred Korzybski

4148   LIFE COMPARED TO A VIOLIN SOLO

Life is like playing a violin solo in public and learning the instrument as one goes on.

Baron Lytton

4149   PROCESS OF LIFE

Life is one long process of getting tired.   *Samuel Butler*

4150   LIVING ONCE

"You can only live once," observed Joe E. Lewis, "but if you live right, once is enough."

4151   DIVERSITY OF CHARACTER

In each human heart are a tiger, a pig, an ass, and a nightingale; diversity of character is due to their unequal activity.   *Ambrose Bierce*

4152   EATING WORDS

Man does not live by words alone, despite the fact that sometimes he has to eat them.   *Adlai Stevenson*

4153   THE WORLD AND YOU

Don't believe the world owes you a living; the world owes you nothing—it was here first.   *Robt. Jones Bindette*

4154   CONFESSIONS

Confessions may be good for the soul but they are bad for the reputation.
                                                                 Thos. Robert Dewar

4155   ERRING

To err is human; to blame it on someone else is even more human.

4156   TROUBLESOME RELATIVES

All people are your relatives, therefore expect only trouble from them.
                                                                    Chinese Proverb

4157   CLIMBING MOLEHILLS

Some people get all their mental exercise by climbing up and down molehills.

MARRIAGE

4158   PUBLIC CONFESSION

Marriage is a ghastly public confession of a strictly private intention.

Ian Hay

4159   ONE INCOME

The trouble with marriage is that a fellow can't support a wife and the government on one income.

4160   HUSBAND'S FACES

All husbands are alike, but they have different faces so we can tell them apart.

4161   QUALITIES OF A WIFE

A man likes his wife to be just clever enough to comprehend his cleverness and just stupid enough to admire it.

4162   EYES, BEFORE AND AFTER MARRIAGE

Keep your eyes wide open before marriage, and half-shut afterwards.

Ben Franklin

4163   WORSHIP AND SACRIFICE

Marriage is when Man worships Woman, and then sacrifices himself at the altar.

4164   COMPATIBILITY

A compatible marriage is one where the man makes the living and the woman makes the living worthwhile.

4165   MAN'S GOVERNMENT

Matrimony is the only state under which every man is free to choose his own form of government—blonde, brunette or redhead.

4166   IDEAL SITUATION

The ideal will be reached when all women are married and all men are single.

4167   BOSS OF HOUSE

Many a man never has to show his wife who's boss in his house—she has a mirror.

4168   A TOAST

May this be one union that will never go on strike!

4169   ANOTHER TOAST

Here's to matrimony—the high seas for which no compass has yet been invented.

4170   AND ANOTHER TOAST

Here's to the man who loves his wife,
  and loves his wife alone.
For many a man loves another man's wife,
  when he ought to be loving his own!

4171   AND STILL ANOTHER TOAST

Here's to our better halves, who reconcile us to our poorer quarters!

MATERNITY

4172   BLAMING THE STORK INSTEAD OF A LARK

A stork is a bird with many things charged against it which should be blamed on a lark.

4173   A TOAST

Here's to the modern mother; she can hold safety pins and a cigarette in her mouth at the same time.

4174   AND ANOTHER TOAST

> Here's to the happiest hours of my life—
> Spent in the arms of another man's wife:
> My Mother!

MEANS

4175   LAYING AN EGG

> A hen is only an egg's way of making another egg.   *Samuel Butler*

MIND

4176   THE WORKING OF THE MIND

> The mind is a wonderful thing. It starts working the minute you're born and never stops until you get up to speak in public.

MODESTY

4177   THE MODEST GIRL

> A modest girl never pursues a man, nor does a mousetrap pursue a mouse.

MONEY AND PRICES

4178   LIVING MONEY

> The money that men make lives after them.   *Samuel Butler*

4179   CYCLES OR CIRCLES

Economists now say we move in cycles instead of running around in circles. It sounds better, but it means the same thing.

4180   THE POOR AND THE RICH

There is only one class in the community that thinks more about money then the rich, and that's the poor.   *Oscar Wilde*

4181   VALUE OF MONEY

Money isn't everything—sometimes it isn't even enough.

4182   CHILDREN AND MONEY

While money isn't everything, it does keep you in touch with your children.

4183   LEARNING THE VALUE OF MONEY

If you would like to know the value of money—go and try to borrow some.
                                                                          Ben Franklin

4184   A FOOL AND HIS MONEY

We know that a fool and his money are very soon parted, but what would be interesting to learn is how they ever got together in the first place.

4185   HOW TO DOUBLE YOUR MONEY

The safest way to double your money is to fold it over once and put it in your pocket.   *K. Hubbard*

4186   SAVINGS FROM YOUR PAY

About the only thing you can save out of your pay these days is—the envelope.

4187   ROLLING DIME

Money doesn't go as far it used to except when the dime rolls under the bed.

4188   TALENT, WORK AND MONEY

If you have talent and work hard and long, anything in the world can be yours —if you have enough money.

4189   WHAT YOU CAN GET FOR A QUARTER

There are still a few things you can get for a quarter—pennies, nickels and dimes!

4190   LIVING IN THE PAST

Living in the past has one thing in its favor—it's cheaper.

4191   MONEY TALKS

Money talks and the first word it learns is "good-bye."

4192   CALLING FOR MONEY

Money may talk, but it is certainly hard of hearing when you call it.

4193   SHRINKING MONEY

Money doesn't go as far as it did, but it stays away just as long.

4194   HISTORY REPEATS ITSELF

The worst thing about history is that it repeats itself, especially about the first of each month.

4195   OLD AND NEW HOTEL SIGNS

The epidemic of expensive hotels has caused most of them to replace the old signs which read, HAVE YOU LEFT ANYTHING? to new ones which ask, HAVE YOU ANYTHING LEFT?

4196   INFLATION AND PREGNANCY

A little inflation is like a little pregnancy—it keeps on growing.

Leon Henderson

4197   A TOAST TO THE GOOD OLD DAYS

A toast to those good old days when Uncle Sam lived within his income—and without most of ours.

4198   ANOTHER TOAST

Blessed are the young for they shall inherit the national debt.

Herbert Hoover

NARROW-MINDEDNESS

4199   BLINDED BY A PIN

He is so narrow-minded that if he fell on a pin, it would blind him in both eyes.

Fred Allen

4200   PEEPING THROUGH KEYHOLE

He was so narrow-minded he could see through a keyhole with both eyes.

Esther Forbes

OBJECTIVITY

4201   TWO SIDES TO EVERY QUESTION

Of course there are two sides to every question, if we really are not interested in either of them.

OBSTETRICIAN

4202   NUMBER OF ASSISTANTS

One of the main reasons an obstetrician is so busy and successful is because he has so many men working for him.

OPPORTUNITY

4203   **OPPORTUNITY OR TEMPTATION?**

Sometimes you don't know who is knocking—opportunity or temptation.

4204   **OPPORTUNITY DISGUISED**

The reason many people fail to recognize opportunity is because it comes disguised as hard work.

ORATORY

4205   **THE ART OF**

Oratory is the art of making deep noises from the chest sound like important messages from the brain.

PESSIMISTS

4206   **FEELINGS OF**

A pessimist is one who feels bad when he feels good for fear he'll feel worse when he feels better.

POISE

4207   **PRESENCE OF MIND**

Poise is the presence of mind to continue talking while the other person picks up the check.

POLITICS

4208   A CONSERVATIVE

A conservative is a man who will not look at the new moon, out of respect for that ancient institution, the old one.   *Douglas Jerrold*

4209   A POLITICAL WAR

A political war is one in which everyone shoots from the lip.
Raymond Moley

4210   PRESENT-DAY POLITICS

In present-day politics, too many people are for either the extreme left or the extreme right. What this country needs is more articulate citizens who are for the extreme middle.

4211   THE STRAW VOTE

A straw vote only shows which way the hot air blows.   *O. Henry*

4212   COMMUNISM VS. CAPITALISM

The Communist, seeing the rich man in his fine home says: "No man should have so much."
The Capitalist, seeing the same thing, says: "All men should have as much."

4213   DEFINITION OF A GOVERNOR

A device attached to a state to keep it from going ahead very fast.

4214   A RADICAL VS. A CONSERVATIVE

A radical is a man with both feet firmly planted in the air. A conservative is a man with two perfectly good legs who has never learned to walk.
F. D. Roosevelt

4215 THE SITTING CONSERVATIVE

A conservative is a man who just sits and thinks, mostly sits.

Woodrow Wilson

4216 ABSENT-MINDED CANDIDATE

Many a candidate who throws his hat into the ring forgets to take his head out.

4217 POLITICIAN'S PLEDGE

When a politician makes a pledge to spend more money he always keeps it.

4218 BURYING THE HATCHET

When opposing groups in a Latin American country bury the hatchet, they both know exactly where it is.

4219 PROS AND CONGRESS

As an example that "pro" is the opposite of "con," the clever student offered: "Progress and Congress."

4220 THE SMALLEST IDEAS

Abraham Lincoln's remark about a well-known politician: "He can compress the most words into the smallest ideas of any man I ever met."

4221 POLITICIANS AND PEOPLE

A clever politician knows that it isn't necessary to fool all of the people all of the time—just during the campaign.

4222 THE BOUGHT POLITICIAN

An honest politician is one who, when he is bought, will stay bought.

Simon Cameron

POVERTY

4223   REMEMBER THE POOR

Remember the poor—it costs nothing.   *Josh Billings*

4224   NUMBER OF POOR PEOPLE

Poverty must have many satisfactions, else there would not be so many poor
people.   *Don Herold*

4225   THE UNINVITED POOR

The poor ye have with ye always—but they are not invited.
                                                        Addison Mizner

PREJUDICE

4226   OPINIONS WITHOUT FACTS

Prejudice is a device that enables you to form opinions without getting the facts.

PROCRASTINATION

4227   THE THIEF OF TIME

Most people put off till tomorrow that which they should have done yesterday.
                                                        Edgar Watson Howe

4228   PLEASURE IN NOT DOING

There is no pleasure in having to do; the fun is in having lots to do and not doing it.   *Mary Wilson Little*

PROPHETS

4229   THE STONED PROPHETS

Prophets were stoned twice—first in anger, then, after their deaths, with handsome slabs in the graveyards.

PROVERBS

4230   THE SHORT AND LONG

A proverb is a short sentence based on long experience.

PUNCTUALITY

4231   A LONELY BELIEVER

I am a believer in punctuality even though it makes me very lonely.

Edward Verrall Lucas

4232   LONELINESS OF

The trouble with being punctual is that nobody's there to appreciate it.

Franklin P. Jones

4233   A VIRTUE

Punctuality is a virtue, if you don't mind being lonely.

PUBLIC SPEAKING

4234   **THE BEGINNING AND THE END**

A speech is like a love affair. Any fool can start it, but to end it requires considerable skill.

Lord Mancroft

4235   **THE COMMAND OF LANGUAGE**

It often shows a fine command of language to say nothing.

4236   **TO AVOID TROUBLE**

One of the best ways to avoid trouble and insure safety is to breathe through your nose. It keeps your mouth shut.

4237   **FREE SPEECH**

A long-winded after-dinner speaker should realize that, while the Constitution may guarantee free speech, it doesn't guarantee listeners.

4238   **THE FIRST TALKING MACHINE**

Edison did not invent the first talking machine. He invented the first one that could be turned off.

4239   **POSITION OF FEET**

Two feet on the ground are worth one in the mouth.

4240   **STRAIGHT-FROM-THE-SHOULDER**

Most of us like a speaker who gives us straight-from-the-shoulder fiery generalities.

4241   **IMPORTANCE OF TIMING**

A public speaker never realizes how important timing is until he notices the audience looking at their watches.

4242 MOUTH OPENED BY MISTAKE

Nothing is opened more by mistake than the mouth.

RELATIVES

4243 THE BEST KIND

Distant relatives are the best kind, and the further the better.
Frank McKinney Hubbard

4244 THE HARDEST THING TO DO

The hardest thing is to disguise your feelings when you put a lot of relatives on the train for home. *Frank McKinney Hubbard*

4245 LONG AND LOUD KNOCKING

If the knocking at the door is unusually long and loud, don't think it is opportunity. It is relatives.

4246 A LONG LIFE

No one lives longer than a rich relative.

SALESMAN

4247 THE ULTIMATE SALESMAN

The ultimate salesman is the guy who can make his wife feel sorry for the girl who lost her compact in his car.

SATISFACTION

4248   CHILDREN AND MONEY

A man with six children is more satisfied than a man with a million dollars, because a man with a million dollars wants more.

SHARING

4249   CAPITALISM VS. SOCIALISM

The inherent vice of capitalism is the unequal sharing of blessings; the inherent virtue of socialism is the equal sharing of misery.   *Winston Churchill*

SELF-DETERMINATION

4250   A HELPING HAND

The man who is looking for a helping hand can always find one—attached to his own arm.

4251   MAKING DREAMS COME TRUE

The best way to make your dreams come true is to wake up.

4252   SOMETHING TO REMEMBER WHEN YOU STUMBLE

Don't worry when you stumble; remember a worm is the only thing that can't fall down.

4253   EXERCISING

Whenever I feel like exercise, I lie down until the feeling passes.
Robert Maynard Hutchins

4254   DANGER IN DOING NOTHING

Between the great things we cannot do and the small things we will not do, the danger is that we shall do nothing.   *Adolph Monod*

4255   WISE MAN VS. SHREWD MAN

A wise man knows everything; a shrewd one, everybody.

4256   SELF-PUNISHMENT

If you could kick the person responsible for most of your troubles, you wouldn't be able to sit down for six months.

SILENCE

4257   SILENCE IS GOLDEN

One way to save face is to keep the lower part of it shut.

SOCIALISM

4258   WORKABLE SOCIALISM

Socialism is workable only in heaven, where it isn't needed, and in hell, where they've got it.   *Cecil Palmer*

SPEECHES

4259   AND BABIES

Speeches are like babies; easy to conceive, hard to deliver.

4260   TELLING AND KNOWING

All too often it takes a speaker twice as long to tell what he thinks as to tell what he knows.

4261   OBJECT OF SPEECH

During the course of most speeches the audience as a rule can figure out what the subject is, but not the object.

4262   BENEFITS OF A GOOD SPEECH

A good speech helps people in several ways. Some rise from it much more knowledgeable. Others wake from it refreshed.

4263   AN IMMORTAL SPEECH

To make a speech immortal, you don't have to make it everlasting.
Lord Leslie Hore-Belisha

4264   THE BEST SPEECH

Speak when you're angry—and you'll make the best speech you'll ever regret.

STORY

4265   LISTENING

Many a person wouldn't listen to your story if he didn't think it was his turn next.

4266 MAKING A LONG STORY SHORT

The best way to make a long story short is to stop listening.

4267 THINKING ALOUD

If you think before you speak, the other fellow gets his joke in first.

Edgar Watson Howe

STRATEGY

4268 KEEP FIRING

When you're out of ammunition, but keep firing.

SUCCESS

4269 AND RELATIVES

Success is relative: The more success the more relatives.

4270 ATTITUDE

Be nice to people on your way up because you'll meet them on your way down.

Wilson Mizner

4271 WINNING

Anybody can win—unless there happens to be a second entry.   *George Ade*

4272 MEETING THE BEST PEOPLE

Early to bed and early to rise, and you will meet very few of our best people.

George Ade

4273   IDEAS OF GREATNESS

He who comes up to his own idea of greatness must always have had a very low standard of it in his mind.   *William Hazlitt*

4274   BLESSED ARE THE BIG WHEELS

Blessed are they who run around in circles, for they shall be known as big wheels.

4275   FACING THE WRONG DIRECTION

The kind of success that turns a man's head always leaves him facing the wrong direction.

4276   THE RABBIT'S FOOT

Depend on the rabbit's foot if you will, but remember it didn't work for the rabbit.   *E. R. Shay*

4277   MINDING ONE'S BUSINESS

The reason why men who mind their own business succeed is because they have so little competition.

4278   SUCCESS OF THE MEEK

It's going to be fun to watch and see how long the meek can keep the earth after they inherit it.   *Frank McKinney Hubbard*

4279   GOING AFTER THINGS

All things come to him who waits, but they come sooner if he goes out to see what's wrong.

TACT

4280   WISH THEY WERE HOME

Tact is the ability to make your guests feel at home where you wish they were.

TAXES

4281   BLOOD MONEY

One of our favorite income tax stories is about the man in a western city who mailed to the collector's office a pint of his blood.

4282   TAXPAYERS' PROTEST

Nothing comes nearer to perpetual motion than the protests of taxpayers.

4283   TAX REVISION

Never put off until tomorrow what you can do today, because by that time there will be a tax on it.

4284   YOU AND THE IRS

You know you can't take it with you, but how do you keep the Internal Revenue Service from taking it from you?

4285   TIGHTENING THE NOOSE

When they close the loopholes in tax legislation, they tighten the noose.

4286   STARVING TAXPAYERS

In this country we let no one starve, but this doesn't necessarily include the taxpayers.

THEORY

4287   A KIND OF HUNCH

A theory is an educated hunch.

TOLERANCE

4288   AND THE RIDICULOUS OPINIONS

A tolerant person is one who is willing to let you have your ridiculous opinions.

TRAINS

4289   HOW TO BE ON TIME

The only way of catching a train I ever discovered is to miss the train before.
Gilbert Keith Chesterton

TROUBLES

4290   NURSING THEM

Troubles, like babies, grow larger by nursing.   *Lady Holland*

TRUST

4291   CUTTING THE CARDS

Trust everybody—but cut the cards.   *Finley Peter Dunne*

TRUTH

4292 **SUPPLY AND DEMAND**

As scarce as truth is, the supply has always been in excess of the demand.

Josh Billings

UTOPIA

4293 **WHEN?**

Conditions that will prevail when Americans enjoy 1950 wages, 1926 dividends, 1932 prices and 1910 taxes.

WAGES

4294 **WHO'S ON TOP?**

A living wage depends upon whether you are getting it or giving it.

WALL STREET

4295 **MAKING IT**

In Wall Street the bulls sometimes make it and the bears sometimes make it, but the hogs never do.

WEALTH

4296   BEING STINGY AND RICH

The reason some people are stingy is also the reason they are rich.

4297   A TOAST

To the idle rich; would to God they were related to us.

WEATHER

4298   AND CONVERSATION

Don't knock the weather; nine-tenths of the people couldn't start a conversation if it didn't change once in a while.   *Frank McKinney Hubbard*

WEIGHT

4299   AND TRAVELING

There is nothing that broadens one like travel, except pastry.

WIDOW

4300   THE LUCKIEST WOMAN

A widow is the luckiest woman in the world. She knows all about men, and all the men who know anything about her are dead.

WOMEN

4301 A DANGEROUS WOMAN

There is no such thing as a dangerous woman; there are only susceptible men.
Joseph Wood Krutch

4302 WOMEN VS. ELEPHANTS

Women are just like elephants to me; I like to look at them, but I wouldn't want one.
Frank McKinney Hubbard

4303 WOMAN'S INTUITION

That uncanny second sense which tells a woman she is absolutely right—whether she is or not.

4304 ADAM'S RIB

I wish Adam had died with all his ribs in his body.

4305 FALLING FOR A WOMAN

Here's to woman! Would that we could fall into her arms without falling into her hands.
Ambrose Bierce

4306 SENSES OF

Women have a wonderful sense of right and wrong, but little sense of right and left.
Don Herald

4307 APPEARANCES

A woman can look both moral and exciting—if she also looks as if it was quite a struggle.
Edna Ferber

4308 NEED FOR WOMEN

Who needs women? I have absolutely no desire for them—except when I see one.
Milt Kamen

4309   A WOMAN PRESIDENT?

The reason women don't run for President is that by the time a woman can decide which hat to throw in the ring, the election is over.

4310   NEVER OLD ENOUGH

No woman is likely to ever be elected President—they never reach the required legal age.

4311   A TIME FOR KISSING

You can't kiss a girl unexpectedly—only sooner than she thought you would.

4312   MAN AND WOMAN

Man has his will, but woman has her way.   *Oliver Wendell Holmes*

4313   BEHAVIOR OF WOMEN

Women do not find it difficult nowadays to behave like men, but they often find it extremely difficult to behave like gentlemen.   *Compton MacKenzie*

4314   THE FINAL DECISION?

A woman's final decision is not necessarily the same as the one she makes later.

4315   A CAREER AND A HOME

A woman can have both a career and a home—if she knows how to put both of them first.

4316   MIDDLE AGE BULGE

Most women will overlook a man's middle age bulge if he's got one in his hip pocket.

4317   THE BEST TEN YEARS

The best ten years in a woman's life come between twenty-eight and thirty.

4318   WOMEN'S MINDS

Women's minds are cleaner than men's—they change them more often.

Oliver Herford

4319   POSITION OF WOMEN

The practice of putting women on pedestals began to die out when men discovered that women could give orders better from that position.

4320   BETTER TIMES

Women have a much better time than men because there are more things forbidden them.

Oscar Wilde

4321   WOMAN AND A GOOD CIGAR

A woman is only a woman, but a good cigar is a smoke.   *Rudyard Kipling*

4322   SILENCE IS GOLDEN

The only golden thing that women dislike is silence.   *Mary Wilson Little*

4323   WOMEN AND WEIGHT

Women are never satisfied. They are trying either to put on weight, take it off or rearrange it.

4324   A MAN'S MISTAKE

Many a man in love with a dimple makes the mistake of marrying the whole girl.   *Stephen Leacock*

4325   INTERESTING FACTS

There is a lot to say in her favor, but the other is more interesting.

Mark Twain

4326   FOOLPROOF INTUITION

Feminine intuition is a fiction and a fraud. It is nonsensical, illogical, emotional, ridiculous—and practically foolproof.

4327   DEFINITION OF A TREE

An object that stands in one place for ages, then leaps in front of a woman who is driving.

4328   THE COST OF A BARGAIN

One of the most difficult tasks in this world is to convince a woman that even a bargain costs money.   *Edgar Watson Howe*

4329   EXPLOSIVE CHARGE

A woman is a creature that's expensive when picked up, but explosive when dropped.

4330   TIME FOR REFLECTION

WIFE—person who will look in a mirror any time—except when she's pulling out of a parking space.

4331   WOMEN CRITICS

A woman who says she can read her husband like a book, and is always furnishing book reviews.

4332   TOAST

To our sweethearts and wives—may they never meet.

4333   ANOTHER TOAST

Here's to God's first thought: Man!
And here's to God's second thought: Woman!
Second thoughts are always best—
So here's to Woman!

4334   AND ANOTHER TOAST

Here's to the ladies—bless them. First in our hearts and first in our pockets.

4335   STILL ANOTHER TOAST

To Woman: the fairest work of creation; the edition being extensive, let no man be without a copy.

4336   AND A FINAL TOAST

Here's to woman—who generally speaking is generally speaking.

WORK

4337   WORKING LIKE HELL

He worked like hell in the country so he could live in the city, where he worked like hell so he could live in the country.   *Don Marquis*

4338   REASON FOR WORKING?

I go on working for the same reason that a hen goes on laying eggs.
                                                                M. L. Mencken

4339   AN ABUNDANCE OF PERFECTION

One searching for an abundance of perfection will find it in applications for employment.

4340   LIFE IS A DIRTY WORD

Life is just a dirty four-letter word: W-O-R-K.

4341   ARRIVAL AND DEPARTURE

I arrive very late at work in the morning, but I make up for it by leaving very early in the afternoon.   *Charles Lamb*

4342   SPARE TIME AND WORK

Work is a fine thing if it doesn't take too much of your spare time.

WORRY

4343   THE CAUSE OF DEATH?

The reason worry kills more people than work is that more people worry than work.

4344   FALLING HAIR

Don't worry if your hair falls out. Suppose it ached and had to be pulled out one at a time, like teeth?

DATE DUE

F			
JUL 1 '74			
JUL 24 '75			
MR 28 '77			
MR 8 '78			
NO 22 '78			
AP 13 '79			
MR 21 '82			
APR 8 '84			
DEC 7 '85			
MAR 23 '88			
DEC 16 '88			
Reserve			
GAYLORD			PRINTED IN U.S.A.